Bitcoin

The beginner 's handbook

Allan Brito

Description and data

Technical info about the Book

Author: Allan Brito

Reference: bitcoinhandbook.com

Edition: 1st

Cover image credits: Allan Brito

First edition date: February 2021

ISBN: 9798706978983

Imprint: Independently published

Help and support: For questions and support about the book content, please visit:

https://www.b3a.pub/contact/

https://bitcoinhandbook.info

This book is an independent production from b3a.pub. Thank you for your support!

About the author

Allan Brito is a Brazilian architect with a passion for open-source and technology. He is an enthusiast of cryptocurrencies and their potential as a disruptive and beneficial financial system evolution.

To spread the word about open-source projects with practical applications in our daily lives, he started the b3a.pub project.

Who should read this book?

If you are trying to find your way around cryptocurrencies and especially Bitcoins, this book is for you! Our goal is to give an introduction to the world of Bitcoin and cryptocurrencies in general.

You don't need any previous experiences with Bitcoin or cryptocurrencies to start using the decentralized currency of the future.

Foreword

If you look at financial headlines in the past couple of years, a name eventually appears with news about record-breaking prices and returns. The word Bitcoin often appears in the news when it hits another record.

During the year 2020, we had economies and countries struggling to handle a pandemic and shattered economies. Even with those terrible events, the year 2020 was incredibly good for Bitcoin. By the end of that year, we saw a movement with big companies placing reasonable amounts of their wealth in Bitcoin.

That move made the price break record after record! It made early investors of Bitcoin incredibly happy and wealthy.

Do you want to start using Bitcoin? It brings a question that many people looking at all those incredible returns have; how does Bitcoin work?

To answer this question, I started to work on this book to teach beginners on the incredible technology behind Bitcoin and how you can use it to save and transfer money. It is a way to get yourself ready to manage a cryptocurrency wallet and understand what happens *under the hood*.

My goal is to make you feel ready and confident on how to manage and use features and assets from cryptocurrency and see how the technology behind Bitcoin can change our world forever.

Welcome to the world of cryptocurrencies!

Allan Brito

February/2021

Bitcoin and cryptocurrencies info

To help you better understand how Bitcoin works and the value associated with the digital currency, we will fix a rate for the asset. During the production of this book, the price of Bitcoin got close to 30,000 USD to 42,000 USD.

To make our lives easier, we will consider the price of Bitcoin as 40,000 USD to make all calculations and conversions in all chapters.

If you want an accurate rate, I strongly suggest you visit any of those sites:

– https://coinmarketcap.com

– https://coingecko.com

Both of them will give you an accurate value for Bitcoin.

Symbols and currencies

To make it easier to understand and track prices and rates, I will use the following symbols to describe monetary values and crypto:

- **USD**: United States Dollar

- **BTC**: Bitcoin

- **ETH**: Ether

- **USDT**: Tether stablecoin

Every time you see one of those acronyms, you can link them to the proper meaning.

Screenshots and wallet addresses

Across the book, you will find multiple examples of addresses for wallets to manage and control Bitcoins. To avoid any potential risk of sending Bitcoins to that address by accident, I changed their seed to make them invalid.

The same applies to screenshots showing addresses that might receive a *blur effect* on both the text address or QR Code.

Disclaimer (Read me first)

A key subject that you must understand and agree on before reading this book is that it has the sole purpose of teaching you about the technology and workflow of Bitcoin. It is not financial advisement in any way. The author of the book is not a financial adviser.

If you need financial advisement, I strongly recommend you to talk to a licensed professional that can give you a proper guidance about the matter.

Risks of managing Bitcoin and cryptocurrencies

Due to the incredible volatility of cryptocurrencies, the risks involved in those financial assets are high, and you should be aware of them before trading Bitcoins. You can either gain or lose a lot of money by trading cryptocurrencies.

Intentionally left blank

TABLE OF CONTENTS

Chapter 01 - What is Bitcoin?

Welcome to the first chapter of our guide about how to start with Bitcoin and cryptocurrencies. Assuming you are starting with the subject and never had any previous experience with Bitcoin, we will give you an overview of cryptocurrency and how it works.

You will learn about the birth of Bitcoin and some of the main advantages of using the cryptocurrency to make payments and store value. One of the benefits of using Bitcoin is that you become the bank and control your financial life, with all the perks and risks.

A critical aspect of Bitcoin that we will start to cover is the incredible price fluctuations. It is one of the most volatile financial assets in the world.

Here is a list of what you will learn in this chapter:

– What is Bitcoin?

– The birth of Bitcoin

– Bitcoin and cryptography

– Bitcoin and privacy

– The past and future of Bitcoin pricing

1.1 What is Bitcoin?

I still remember my first experiences managing my own money when I was a child, which consisted of asking money for my parents and grandparents to buy candy and comic books. At that time, my goals and objectives were easy to achieve. With a couple of coins, I could easily get back home with a pocket full of candy and two of my favorite comic books.

As you grow older, the financial goals evolve, and you probably moved from candy and comic books to real estate, cars, smartphones, and more. That requires a lot more than a couple of coins to buy. That statement about coins would be true if said in the early 2000s, but something changed around 2009. With the right type of coin, you can buy a lot of things with "a couple."

What happened that year? In 2009, we saw the beginning of an evolution in how we deal with money with the first cryptocurrency release, Bitcoin. What is Bitcoin? The most straightforward answer to that question is to say Bitcoin is a digital currency. Unlike other familiar currencies like the United States Dollar, we don't have any central bank or country behind Bitcoin (Figure 1.1).

Figure 1.1 - *Bitcoin logo*

Here are a few of the main characteristics of Bitcoin:

– Decentralized

– Private

– Secure

– Peer-to-peer

Those are only some of the main features of Bitcoin, and later we will enlist more aspects of the coin.

When looking carefully at Bitcoin, you immediately see similarities with physical currencies mixed with the digital world's unique characteristics. For instance, you can "store" those Bitcoins in a digital wallet and break each coin into smaller parts to mimic the behavior of a physical currency, in a similar way to what we do with the Dollar, where we have paper bills and coins.

Info: *The smaller division of a Bitcoin is 0.00000001 BTC with the nickname of satoshi. You can also refer to that unit as 1 Sat.*

The similarities between a quarter dollar coin and a quarter of a Bitcoin are only numeric because, regarding the value, it is wildly different. I don't have to explain the value of a quarter dollar because you are probably familiar with what you can buy with that amount. What about 0.25 BTC?

As of today, you can convert 0.25 BTC to around USD 8,000.00, which is insane when you think about the evolution of this currency. Just recently, Bitcoin broke again another record with its value hitting a record of 42,000.00 USD to 1 BTC.

The year 2020 was incredibly difficult for all major economies globally because of COVID19, and things were also hard for investors. That was not the case for people holding Bitcoins. From January to December of 2020, we saw an increase of almost 400% in the value of Bitcoin.

That is why people start looking to Bitcoin as an important asset to invest in the long term. A digital currency could quickly become a pillar of a revolution in how we manage, spend, and save money.

To better understand the benefits and risks of Bitcoin, we will explain several of the aspects of this currency in the next chapters of the book. We can now define Bitcoin as a digital currency that exists only in computers and the "digital realm."

Info: With Bitcoin, we saw the birth of a currency based on cryptography that spawned several other coins. Those coins receive the name of AltCoins or Alternative coins. There are more than 8000 types of Altcoins available.

1.2 The birth of Bitcoin

When and who created Bitcoin? If you do a quick search to find the creator of Bitcoin, you get Satoshi Nakamoto's name as the creator and father of the currency. That is what official records show. From his name, you probably might think that Bitcoin is a creation of a Japanese researcher. However, Satoshi Nakamoto's name is most likely an alias for a different person or group of people.

The truth is that no one knows for sure who is behind Satoshi Nakamoto's identity. Why the secrecy? If you try to start a parallel currency that competes with a government and has no regulation, it will probably raise red flags on financial authorities. Due to the project's nature, he decided to stay anonymous and use the alias Satoshi Nakamoto.

1.2.1 The first appearance of Bitcoin

In August 2008, a white paper describing how Bitcoin works appeared in a cryptography mailing list with the title of *Bitcoin: A Peer-to-Peer Electronic Cash System*. The Bitcoin network went live in January 2009, and Satoshi Nakamoto himself made the first transaction with a reward of 50 BTC.

Info: As you will notice along with the book, we will eventually describe a reward for Bitcoin transitions. Why is there a reward for transitions? We will describe it in detail when we talk about Mining in Chapter 6.

From that point, we started to see people using Bitcoins to make transitions with a slow pace and reception. Most of the people trading and using Bitcoin were enthusiasts of digital currencies. It wasn't mainstream like today, where we can easily find news regarding Bitcoin prices and adoption online.

Bitcoins' first documented trade in history was a transaction between two users from the Bitcoin forums with a value of 10,000 BTC to buy two pizzas. It was 2009, and the Bitcoin price was close to zero.

How much is that worth today? Those two pizzas worth 320 Million USD today. That is what you get with 10,000 BTC. If you want to check the history, here is the link to the pizza discussion:

```
https://bitcointalk.org/index.php?topic=137.0
```

What about Satoshi Nakamoto? The person using the alias was still active in the Bitcoin forums until 2013 and suddenly stopped posting messages. His real identity remains a mystery until today, with several people trying to link Satoshi Nakamoto to people in the cryptology field and financial business.

Why did he disappear from the forums? Many people believe that due to the increased popularity of Bitcoin, he thought it would be better to stay away from any possible breakdown on the currency creators.

1.3 Bitcoin and cryptography

As you probably notice from our description about the birth of Bitcoin, it appeared for the first time in a mailing list dedicated to cryptography. The reason for that has a direct relation to how Bitcoin works. Are you familiar with cryptography? What is it? The easiest way to describe cryptography is to say it is a method of protecting information, usually with a code or key to hide information.

If you want to send a message to someone and don't want other people to understand the meaning of that message, you can use a code to hide its real purpose. One of the most effective ways of creating such codes and keys is with math.

You don't have to be a mathematician to start using cryptography in your daily life. Even a small and simple task can use cryptography concepts. For instance, you might be with your family during dining, and you have to speak to a brother about the surprise birthday present to your mother.

How to say that to everyone when your mother is also present? You can previously define that you will refer to the present as "investment" in any conversation. That will be the key to understand all messages.

Once at the table, you can easily say that you have a great "investment" in mind, and you will probably make a move the next day. Everyone at the table with the key will understand that you found the present. Tomorrow is the day to buy it. With no knowledge of the key, the mother doesn't know the real meaning of the message.

We use cryptography every day on our phones or talk with people in apps with an encrypted connection. Even on the web, when you browse sites with an "HTTPS" header, it means we have an encrypted connection. It is part of our daily lives, and Bitcoin considers that.

Of course, when talking about complex cryptography, we have much more than a simple word replacement to hide data. At that level, you find math equations protecting sensitive data. Some military-grade cryptography involves math requiring thousands of hours from powerful computers to solve each equation.

With Bitcoin, we have a high-level complexity regarding cryptography. The math behind it is complex enough to stress powerful computers for hours to process new coins and validate transaction security.

1.3.1 What makes a Bitcoin unique?

As a child, you might have a brilliant idea for getting more money and solve your immediate and future financial problems. Since money is a type of paper, you could easily print more money to fulfill your needs! It can be a solution in a child's mind, but aside from being illegal, you will also face problems when trying to use currency not issued by a central bank or government.

Only a couple of companies backed by the government and central banks hold the right to print money. A central bank can print as much money as they want, and sometimes they might have to print more to finance government debt. That is usually not a good idea, but they have the means to print as much money as they want.

What about Bitcoin? Now that it is worth several thousand dollars, it would be great to sit on my computer and use a copy and paste tool to make unlimited Bitcoins. Unfortunately, it doesn't work that way. To ensure that Bitcoins have a limited supply and people can't simply make copies of them, we have an ingenious method to create each digital coin.

Each Bitcoin is a result of a complex math calculation derived from a cryptography algorithm. That is how you validate that a Bitcoin is real. How do you validate that a Dollar bill is real? You can look at several aspects of the bill:

– Paper type

– Serial number

– Watermark

Those are a few of the safety measurements that central governments take to ensure people can only get their money from a central location. When you go to a bank to deposit money, the teller can easily check those aspects of the money to verify if it is real.

What about Bitcoins? How to verify if they are real? A group of computers in the network verifies if the math solution to that equation is real. If it matches, the Bitcoin is valid.

Who makes this verification? Here is one of the genius ideas behind Bitcoin. The verification of each coin happens in the Bitcoin network among all users. Each computer in the network receives the name of node. It is a peer-to-peer technology (P2P). There is no central computer or company behind the network. It is open to any person to join.

1.3.2 How to create a Bitcoin?

This is all interesting but doesn't answer the main question: how to create new Bitcoins?

The creation of new Bitcoins happens with a process called mining. It is part of the verification of each transaction in the Bitcoin network. For instance, when you try to send Bitcoins to someone else, the transaction needs confirmation. Several computers with the Bitcoin software connected to the network verify if those Bitcoins can move between those persons.

A miner picks a group of various transactions called a block and process them. He collects a reward as new Bitcoins, or fractions of a coin, for helping with the network.

Info: You can imagine a block as a list with dozens of transactions with the sender, recipient, and fee. It would be like if a bank teller had to do all those transactions by hand. Once he processes all transactions, the network grants a reward.

The miner also gets a small fee based on that verification for each transaction. In the early days of the Bitcoin network, the rewards were massive, like receiving 20 or 10 BTC by each block. Of course, at the time, the value of each Bitcoin was close to nothing. Today, each verification awards only tiny fractions of a coin.

To mine a block, you need a computer fast enough to process a series of math calculations. Once you get a solution to the math, you receive a Bitcoin token. Over time the equation becomes more complex, and it is harder to get new tokens.

Can we create and earn infinite Bitcoins? There is today a cap imposed by Satoshi Nakamoto of 21 million Bitcoins. It can't go beyond that amount. Once we hit that limit, you will only gain new Bitcoins by validating transitions with the fee transactions and no rewards from miming blocks.

Unlike central governments that can print an unlimited amount of cash, we only have a limited Bitcoins supply. That is one of the reasons the coins are valuable.

In the current rate of Bitcoin generation, the last Bitcoin will appear sometime around years 2140-2150. Today we have about 18 million Bitcoins in the network, and since it becomes harder and harder to receive tokens, the creation rate decreases over time.

Info: There are still 3 million Bitcoins waiting to "born." How much is that in Dollars? Around 96 Billion USD worth of Bitcoins with current exchange rates.

1.4 Bitcoin and privacy

At the beginning of Bitcoin, we had very few people seeing it as a form of investment or a valuable asset. A segment of society embraced technology to evade the eyes of authorities from their financial activities. I'm talking about organized crime and people doing illegal activities saw in Bitcoin a way of business that was under the radar of law enforcement.

The main reason for that has a relation to the private aspect of each transaction in the network.

In a traditional bank, you have your money and assets with strong regulatory oversight from both the government and law enforcement. It helps protect the funds and also gives the government power to keep track of your financial activities. It has both positive and negative sides in this regard.

For instance, several countries offer some type of protection to money deposited in a bank. In the United States, we have the Federal Deposit Insurance Corporation (FDIC) that can secure deposits up to 250,000 USD if the bank goes out of business.

On the other hand, you can't hide your financial activities from regulators. If you receive a huge deposit of 500,000 USD in your account, it will at least require you to pay taxes over that amount. In a more suspicious behavior, it can raise red flags in law enforcement.

The tracking of financial activities is a problem if your government wants to control your life beyond finances.

It might be a problem in countries with limited personal freedom. For instance, you might want to buy a Bible. In some countries in the world, the possession of a Bible is illegal. If you buy it with Bitcoins, no one can track that transaction.

With Bitcoin, you are the bank, and it is hard to track who is behind each transaction.

A bank account usually holds information like:

– Name

– Address

– Social security number or Tax ID

That can easily tie the money to a person or institution. With Bitcoin, you don't have any idea who is making a transaction. It is all a collection of numbers and digital addresses.

Using Bitcoins as their primary currency for everyday transitions, a person could easily evade any oversight from financial institutions and law enforcement. It is a completely private transaction that disclosure a person's identity.

Info: Later in the book, we will disclose how we can somehow track Bitcoin transactions.

Since doing those transactions with Bitcoins doesn't raise any red flags from the government, most the organized crime embraced Bitcoins in the early days.

It is also convenient to do business with a digital currency. Criminals changed the handling of large amounts of cash to Bitcoins. That is a huge problem when you think about the logistics. Just think about the burden of storing and moving sums like 500,000 USD or more to close a "deal."

For that reason, you still find people today that associate Bitcoin with illegal activities. It has a history of use by people and organizations with no interest in investments but instead hides their business.

1.4.1 The Silk Road case

A famous case that was all over the media in the early days of Bitcoin was the Silk Road marketplace. It was shut down by law enforcement around 2013, and it was a place that people used to trade all sorts of illegal products. What was the may currency used by the marketplace? They were using Bitcoin to avoid any type of detection from the government.

In a recent move, the United States government seized a total of 70,000 BTC from wallets associated with the Silk Road marketplace. That is worth today to about 2,300,500,000 USD. Remember that back in 2013, Bitcoin value was infinitely lower than it is today.

1.4.2 Bitcoin and digital crime

Since the use of Bitcoin offers an unprecedented level of privacy, it opened opportunities for new types of digital felonies. A problem that many companies and people face today is what we call a ransomware attack. In this type of event, you are asked to pay the ransom in Bitcoins.

What is a ransomware attack? In such attacks, a person or a group breaks into the network of a business and encrypt their data. You lose access to all data in the network. Instead of your data, you see a message asking you to buy and send Bitcoins to an address to get a key to recover access to the system.

Using Bitcoin, the people behind the attack can do that at a safe distance, and no payment will be traced back to them. If you do a quick search in the media, you will find several examples of such attacks in:

– Hospitals

– Industries

– Tech companies

As part of each news piece, the description usually mentions the requirement of payments made with Bitcoin.

1.4.3 Bitcoin to overrule financial restrictions

Another type of news that we often find when looking at finances and politics is a trade and financial sanctions on countries. It can happen due to several reasons, and it tries to enforce certain politics by a nation or group. If you put yourself as the ruler of one of those nations or companies with financial restrictions, you can easily figure out a way of overruling those limitations with Bitcoin.

You can get Bitcoins from a location where you don't have any restrictions and do business with anyone around the world, regardless of regulators or institutions. At the same time, it is a way to keep trading regardless of sanctions but also frightening to think about what a hostile nation could do with such freedom.

That is one of the reasons many countries today still ban anything related to cryptocurrencies like Bitcoin. If you live in a country with a policy of full control over their population, they will most likely try to make you stay away from Bitcoin. Remember that it is a network offering overall private transactions, which is terrifying for some governments.

1.5 Bitcoin pricing

One aspect of Bitcoin that is a mystery for a lot of people the pricing of each coin. What is the base to set the pricing of Bitcoins? This is another unique aspect of digital currency, a model ruled by offer and demand only. Since we don't have any central banks or institutions controlling or managing Bitcoin rates, we have considerable fluctuations in shorts amounts of time.

When we have more people trying to buy coins than selling, the price goes up—the opposite results in a drop.

The pricing of Bitcoin is famous for fluctuations that show gains or losses of 25% in a matter of days. It is a highly volatile financial asset.

1.5.1 Comparing Bitcoin trading and the Stockmarket

To better understand the offer and demand model, we can make a quick comparison between Bitcoins and a well-established form of investment, which are stocks. What is the main driver behind stock prices? You can name a few factors to set stock prices:

- Demand

- Profit expectation

- Business performance

Those are just a few of the factors that could impact stock pricing. As you can see from the list, we have demand as one of the factors. It works like any product that has limited supply and high demand. A seller can ask for higher prices when it finds many people trying to buy a product. As a result, we get price increases.

Unlike Bitcoin trading, stock markets have strong regulations where you find mechanisms to protect investors when things go wrong, like the "circuit breaker." This rule is useful when we have something called panic selling.

A trader might start to sell an asset when he sees everyone in the market trying to get rid of a particular share. As a result, more people will see that as a sign that something is not right and will also try to sell. With supply and demand in place, the price of that stock falls sharply.

When something like that happens, we have "panic selling." As a result, we have lots of people trying to sell and a few of them buying. With more offers than demand, we got huge price drops. Once the drop hits a certain level, the "circuit breaker" takes place. It halts all trading until people calm down.

Do we have a "circuit break" in Bitcoin trading? Like we mentioned before, there is no regulation in Bitcoin trading. For that reason, when something happens, and the price must go down, we see some real panic. That is why we can see huge gains or losses in short periods.

An example of that happens between 2017 and 2018. During the year 2017, we saw one of the biggest "bull runs" in the Bitcoin pricing history. Across 2017 the price went from 1,200 USD to almost 20,000 USD during that year. Anyone with an investment in Bitcoins in early 2017 and kept those coins until late December experienced gains of 1,800%.

After that long "bull run" we had at the beginning of the following year, an event would easily trigger a "circuit breaker" with Bitcoin pricing dropping almost 50% in two weeks by February of 2018. What caused the price drop? Among the factors, we have lots of people with coins trying to cash out and sell their assets. With more people trying to sell than buyers, the prices went down.

Info: Some other factors like the release of new Alternative Coins contributed to the fluctuation. A few of those Altcoins offers something called ICO (Initial Coin Offer) to gather funds for a project. People buy the coins expecting it to become the next Bitcoin. After the ICO, certain projects were almost abandoned, which hurt the trust in cryptocurrencies in general.

If you want to start investing in Bitcoins, you must know that huge price fluctuations are normal and will eventually happen. There is no "circuit break" to halt trading and lower those gains or losses. It is supply and demand in its raw state with no regulations or oversight.

At the moment, a lot of people think that Bitcoin is in a long "bull run" that is lasting for several months. How long will it last? No one knows.

When you think about pricing, we get a similar relation between Bitcoins and stocks with a supply and demand relation. At its core, while we find more people willing to acquire Bitcoins than holders trying to sell, prices will keep climbing.

Info: What is a "bull run"? That is a term used in the stock markets to identify a period where stocks have gains over extended periods.

1.5.2 The dark side of money

In section 1.4, we mentioned the "dark side" of Bitcoins and their use by people trying to evade law enforcement's eyes to do all sorts of criminal activities. That doesn't mean that Bitcoin is the only way people with bad intentions find to break the law. If you look at all potential financial fraud and felonies, you will see that it has a history dating much longer than Bitcoins.

Using the Stockmarket as a comparison again, we can name one simple example of financial fraud in this type of trading. Have you ever heard of the term "insider trading"? It happens when someone with privileged information on the matter tries to sell or buy shares.

For instance, you might be aware that a certain high-profile company had a terrible year on sales, and it will release that information to the public in two weeks. It will certainly make the price of the company shares drop. If you have shares from this company, you can start selling them regularly and avoid losses. That way, you can make someone else with no privileged information lose the money instead of you.

You can also do the same with an expectation of huge gains. For instance, a company with a revolutionary product may prepare for a public announcement in a couple of weeks. If you have access to that information, you could start buying shares today to sell them after the announcement.

All those examples are cases of "inside trading" in the stock markets and would probably raise red flags on regulators.

There are multiple examples of fraud cases using stocks and financial investments that showed themselves as Ponzi schemes across the years. It means that you will find people with bad intentions everywhere, and Bitcoin is not their only playground. When talking about investments, you always get a risk factor of losing some of the investment.

Info: A Ponzi scheme is a popular form of financial fraud, where you get people to invest money in an asset. The fraud consists of taking money from people that are joining the scheme to pay early investors. It also receives the name of investment pyramid.

1.6 Forget the past. Aim for the future

Many people looking at Bitcoins today as a form of investment will start to do a type of "mental math" after looking to prices getting close to 42,000 USD. What if I had 10 Bitcoins today? Wouldn't that be great? It is a valid exercise for investors to project it mentally and aiming for future gains.

Looking at the history of pricing for a particular asset before an investment is something that everyone should do before putting your money on anything. This works for financial markets, real estate, or any type of investment. For instance, if you plan to buy a house as an investment, it is a wise decision to check price history.

When dealing with stocks, you will find all financial reports with recommendations to buy or sell certain shares. They even point to a target price to buy or sell. To create such reports, you have multiple factors taking place, including the price history analysis.

As soon as you take a look at the price history of Bitcoin, you start to wonder what if you acquire the coins back when it was worth close to nothing. One of the best periods to get Bitcoins was in 2011 when it was in parity with the United States Dollar. One Bitcoin was equivalent to one Dollar.

A simple investment of 200 USD in 2011 would worth millions of dollars today. That is an interesting mental exercise but could easily lead to anxiety and pressure to get results. People who acquired coins at that time and hold them until today enjoy some impressive returns for the investment.

Info: *Among the community of Bitcoin investors, you will usually find the word "HODL" as a reference to holding the coins despite price fluctuations. People usually ask themselves; should I sell or "hodl"?*

1.6.1 Future of Bitcoin pricing

As mentioned before, we have huge fluctuations in pricing, and things could go up or down quickly. It is wise to look at the price history and learn about Bitcoin trading behavior and prepare yourself for long term investments. But, if you don't plan to start day trading or expect quick returns, it is also wise not to look at price changes.

As in any type of investment, you should prepare for good times and bad times regarding pricing evolution. If you have plans to save for college, retirement, or anything with a long term perspective, it will be wise to keep calm and hold your coins. Or, like the Bitcoin enthusiasts would say, "hodl" the coins.

Today we have a massive influx of people starting to use Bitcoin as protection over market fluctuations and inflation. After all the problems we faced in 2020, it is even harder to get good returns on investments with interest rates close to zero in many markets. People who bet on Bitcoins in the past couple of years are getting the rewards over their initial investment now—after several months and years holding the coins.

We can, once again, make a comparison with investments in the Stockmarket. There, you must follow a simple rule to ensure you have gained. You should buy when shares are cheaper and sell them when the price increases. It is simple math that works fine for Stocks but is hard to apply to Bitcoins.

By the time I'm writing this book, the Bitcoin prices break record after record and are close to 42,000 USD for 1 BTC. A couple of days ago, it was also with an all-time high at around 30,000 USD. In just two weeks, it went from a record to something even higher.

What was my reaction when I saw the prices hitting 30,000 BTC? I bought more. Unlike stocks, it is impossible to set a maximum price for Bitcoin. When people see the headlines of Bitcoin breaking new records of value, they will start to buy it! Then supply and demand take control.

If I was following the Stockmarket rule and waited for prices to drop, I would lose a lot of gains from the price spikes. One of Bitcoin trading's challenging aspects is that we don't have a ceiling or limit for gains. Today's price might be a record, which will easily be cheap in 1 month. It is particularly hard to predict those prices.

As I usually recommend for anyone that asks me about Bitcoin as a long-term investment, you should forget about the past and aim for the future.

What is next?

As you probably noticed from this last chapter, I mentioned multiple times the Bitcoin pricing rollercoaster. By the time I'm writing this book, it was around 32,000 and 35,000 USD. How is it today? As a way to get you used to the price changes, you should start to eventually check rates.

Multiple locations give you a history of Bitcoin pricing. A great resource to find a list with important data regarding cryptocurrencies is:

https://coinmarketcap.com

You find a list with a ranking of the most active coins in the market by volume of transactions and price. What coin has the biggest market cap? Of course, it is Bitcoin from a large margin.

Get ready to start managing your Bitcoins!

Chapter 2 - How Bitcoin and the Blockchain work?

The use of a cryptocurrency like Bitcoin is an amazing technological feature, which raises questions like; how does it work? What is behind Bitcoin? In this chapter, we will start to discuss one of the most prominent technologies powering Bitcoin. Have you ever heard of the word Blockchain?

That is by far one of the biggest contributions related to the digital money field, with applications transcending our finances. Today we can easily find projects using Blockchains for many different purposes.

You will learn more about how the Blockchain technology works and also compare it t a traditional banking system and how it can ensure the safety and reliability of the Bitcoin network.

Here is a list of what you will learn:

– How Bitcoin works

– Relation between Bitcoins and the Blockchain

– How the Blockchain works

– Tools to explore the Blockchain

– The irreversible nature of a Blockchain

– Security behind a Blockchain

2.1 How Bitcoin works?

Chapter one discussed some aspects of how Bitcoin works, like the extensive use of cryptography to process and link each coin and transaction to a complex math operation. That way, you ensure that no one can easily create new coins or validate transactions out of nowhere.

Another key aspect of Bitcoins is the decentralized nature, which doesn't use any central server or government to operate. It is an open-source and democratic network that allows anyone with a computer and an internet connection to participate. That is what we call a peer-to-peer network.

2.1.1 The centralized bank structure

Those are the technology-related aspects, but what about the finances? If we start to think about a traditional bank account and compare it with Bitcoin, we immediately start to wonder about some common bank "features" and how it works in Bitcoin. For instance, how do I see an account statement? Is there a balance? How the network keeps track of transactions?

Traditional brick and mortar banks have computer systems using centralized databases to keep track of all transactions. If you make a deposit or a purchase from your checking account, a record appears in your account statement, and it goes to the bank database.

If you are not familiar with databases, we can think about them as a specialized type of computer data that stores information. It works like a spreadsheet where you can insert all types of information. Unlike the spreadsheet that works great for a single person, a database can receive multiple interactions and offers better performance.

The database also helps the bank to keep track of your balance and confirm transactions. For instance, you can go to a grocery store and buy some coffee with your Debit card. Assuming you have a balance of 10 USD in your account and the coffee costs 5 USD, the bank system compares your balance to the purchase cost. If you have enough money in the balance, the system approves the purchase.

All the process happens almost in real-time. Just to give you an idea of how many transactions one card company can process, it can go up to 65,000 transactions per second.

Since we are talking about a corporation with a huge demand for infrastructure, they need a location to keep that database running nonstop like a warehouse and manage backups, security, and maintenance. Every time you open the bank app or site, you make a request to that database to manage your accounts.

Info: *That is a simplification of a bank system because most of the time, a bank runs multiple servers in different locations as a redundancy. But, it still has sole control over the structure.*

2.1.2 Bitcoin decentralisation

How can we compare Bitcoin to a traditional bank? It goes in the opposite direction. Unlike a traditional bank with a central database and server with all your records and balance, with Bitcoin, we find a decentralized network that is both open and free to join.

The Bitcoin network is responsible for validating transactions and manage all aspects of how you use digital currency. For instance, if you try to spend the coins to buy something, the network will authorize you and confirm the transaction to the seller.

Another common task of the Bitcoin network is to confirm your balance. It will check if you have the coins for any given transaction.

One of the core aspects of the Bitcoin network is its peer-to-peer nature. All transactions happen between ordinary computers in the network and not a central server from a bank. The peer-to-peer (P2P) technology is famous as a file sharing service with people transferring files between computers online. In the Bitcoin case, it is a way of maintaining a network of computers called nodes running the system.

Each node has a full copy of the Bitcoin ledger, and they compare records between each node. That way, a single person can't change the ledger to create fraudulent transactions. If a single person tries to make a change, the other nodes reject the change.

When you do a transaction with Bitcoin, it goes into the network and gets distributed to computers worldwide for validation. If multiple nodes confirm the transaction, you have a successful operation. The Bitcoin network uses a technology called Blockchain.

With the Blockchain, we have financial records and transactions that are not in a central location but spread across thousands of nodes. A node of the network is useful for:

– Mine new Bitcoins

– Validate transactions

– Keep track of all transactions in the network

Since we have the networks running in a collaborative environment, with nodes spread across the world, we can easily state that it is the opposite of a bank. It doesn't have a central location, and you can't shut it down. If a node goes off-line, we have hundreds of others keeping the network active.

2.2 Bitcoins and the Blockchain

If you try to ask anyone about how a bank works, they can probably give you a rough explanation about how they can deposit money for safekeeping. When it is time to spend the money, they verify if you have the balance and transfer it to the seller of a product or service. Of course, It is more complicated than that, but it is an easy workflow that most people understand.

What about the Blockchain in the Bitcoin network? How does it work? First of all, what is a Blockchain, and why it receives that name?

To make it easier for you to understand the Blockchain, we can compare it with an accountant. Imagine that this accountant has several books to keep track of the flow of cash for their clients.

Each one of those books has the following features:

– 100 pages

– Can record 1000 transactions

– On the cover, they have a sequential number for each week of the year

For instance, at the beginning of January, the accountant picks the book with "Week 1" and records all transactions. He fills all the pages until Sunday. The following week he starts filling the next book with "Week 2" on the cover. While using the book for the second week, he puts the book for the previous week in a safe location.

By following this methodology, he will have a book for each week after a few months.

Since the accountant can eventually make a mistake in the process of adding records, we can make the comparison even better by adding two additional accountants in different cities. They all follow the same procedure:

1. Get a book labeled for each week of the year

2. Add records for transactions of their clients

3. After each week, they file the book and get a new one

4. At the end of each week, or cycle, they get onto the phone to compare each one records

The last step of comparing records is a safeguard to ensure they have the most accurate information. If one of the books has a mistake, we can easily use the other two accountants' records to make a quick correction.

A system like the one described is easy to understand because it uses real examples with people and physical objects in our daily lives, like notebooks.

2.2.1 From paper to Blockchain

What about the Blockchain? A Blockchain is a type of database that can store information in blocks. Each block has a position in a long chain of information. Once a block becomes full, it goes to the general ledger of transactions and is chained with all previous blocks.

Our example with the accountants can easily describe the Blockchain:

– Three accountants to record transactions = *Multiple nodes of the Bitcoin network recording transactions*

– Accountants in multiple locations = *Nodes available globally in any computer with the Bitcoin software*

– Books for every week of the year = *Blocks of information that once become full goes to the chain in chronological order*

– If an error appears in the records, it is easy to fix using the other books = *If data gets corrupted or changed, a fix is easily available with the use of other blocks in the chain*

The Blockchain is an incredible way of adding a level of security and control over transitions and is one of the strongest features of Bitcoin. When you think about traditional banks, an aspect that is part of their business is trust. If you don't trust a bank, you probably won't leave your money there. The same applies to the Bitcoin Blockchain. It is a reliable way of managing a currency and much more.

Later in the chapter, we will discuss the security aspects of the Blockchain and why you should trust it to keep a record of your cryptocurrencies.

2.3 How the Blockchain works?

The core concept of a Blockchain as a way to store data wasn't born with the Bitcoin protocol and dated almost twenty years early. It was with the proposal from the mythic Satoshi Nakamoto that we saw their implementation in a digital currency.

In the previous section, we described an example with three accountants that try to mimic a Blockchain workflow. Now that you are more familiar with the process, we can go into more details. Like mentioned earlier, the main purpose of the Blockchain is to keep track of all transactions in the Bitcoin network. It is the Bitcoin ledger.

For instance, when someone tries to send a Bitcoin to another person, the transaction must be verified by the network. We can call the person sending Bitcoins as the sender and another one the receiver. Let's imagine that the sender is trying to transfer 5 BTC.

How does the Blockchain confirm each transaction?

Here is a basic workflow:

1. The network verifies in the Bitcoin ledger if the sender has a balance of 5 BTC or more

2. If positive, it transfers the amount to the address provided in the transaction

3. Other nodes receive the same data for confirmation

4. The network nodes come to a consensus that it is a legitimate transaction

5. After multiple confirmations, the sender receives a notification that it now has a 5 BTC deposit

6. All other nodes receive the information about the new balance for both sender and receiver

That is the Bitcoin ledger's core behavior, and it keeps track of all coins and transactions.

Info: If you want to join the Blockchain to help with the verification process of transactions, you must download the entire record of blocks to contribute to the network.

In this example, we described two subjects managing the transaction as the sender and receiver. Do they appear in the Blockchain records? Yes, you can see them in the records but unlike a traditional bank where you can easily track an account by:

– Account and routing numbers

– SWIFT or IBAN

A Bitcoin transaction appears with the identification of a digital wallet associated with the transaction. Only the flow from one location to the other appears. How owns each wallet? No one knows, and it is virtually impossible to find that information from the Bitcoin ledger.

Unlike a traditional bank that requires several documents to open a checking account, you don't even have to provide an email address to get a digital wallet to manage Bitcoins. It is a private operation. It is one of the highlights of the process and what makes people adopt Bitcoin and other cryptocurrencies. A completely private way of managing your financial life.

Info: The address used in transactions has a name of Public Key.

2.4 Exploring the Blockchain

Blockchain technology is an incredible way of ensuring you are doing financial operations with Bitcoins securely and reliably. It also offers an innovative and unprecedented way of open access to the network's transition history and backlog. How does that work?

Imagine for a second that you gained access to a unique section of your bank system where you can view all the transitions made by account holders in real-time. You can sneak into other people's accounts. For instance, when someone goes to a gas station and uses a card, you can see the transaction.

If something like that happened to a traditional bank, it would be a massive security breach to the bank. Would you open an account with that bank if you knew that someone else could have access to your financial life? Probably not.

What if I told you that you can do that with the Bitcoin ledger? As mentioned before, the Blockchain and the entire Bitcoin network are open. It also means you can view and search the entire history of transactions. When someone makes a transaction with Bitcoin, it appears in the public ledger, and anyone can view details about the transaction.

Is that a massive security breach? If we were talking about a traditional bank system, it would be a scandal. But, since the Blockchain keeps everything private, you don't have any way of knowing who is making the transaction. It is all a collection of numbers and symbols.

A resource that I like to use and recommend for people unfamiliar with the Blockchain is an explorer. There you can track and view records of current and past transactions. Those are some of the most popular Blockchain explorers:

– https://www.blockchain.com

– https://blockchair.com

– https://btc.com

They offer an easy way for anyone to view transactions and addresses from the Bitcoin network. You can see all types of transactions in the network, from someone saving for college or high-profile movements of millions of Dollars.

All you need to track those transactions is a Public key from a wallet.

It is a fun way of spending some time getting familiar with the Blockchain, trying to imagine the purpose of each of the high-value transactions. From time to time, we can see massive amounts of coins changing wallets with transactions of 50 BTC or more. Is it some millionaire investing in Bitcoins? A foreign country that is forbidden from doing business selling oil? It is impossible to know, but an interesting way to see how the network is alive and working 24/7.

Info: *Regarding cryptocurrencies and investment, we usually call those players managing millions of dollars in assets and Bitcoins as "whales".*

2.5 The Blockchain is irreversible

An aspect of our daily financial lives that gives us some peace of mind when doing something with a certain risk level is that you can reverse a financial transaction if needed. That is a typical operation with credit cards and has a name of "chargeback."

For instance, you might buy something online, and the seller doesn't ship in time or doesn't ship at all. When it happens, we can usually call the credit card company or the bank and ask for a chargeback. With enough information, the card company will cancel the purchase and charge the seller.

It is also an important measure to mitigate fraud and cases where people to your financial data like credit card numbers. With those pieces of information, a person could start to spend online using your identity. If the card company system doesn't detect the fraud and deny those transitions, it will probably reverse them later.

What about Bitcoin transactions? Can we reverse them in case we have a similar problem? Short answer: no. Once you confirm a transaction with Bitcoins and it is in the Blockchain, the process is irreversible. There is one way only to reverse a transaction, but it would require a massive amount of work and money.

To better understand the hypothetical way of reversing a transaction, we can start by defining some nodes. Imagine that we have today about 50,000 active nodes in the Bitcoin network. Each one of those nodes has a copy of the Blockchain with a full history of transitions.

Because each node in the network keeps a copy of the Blockchain, to rollback a transaction, you will have to edit and change the Blockchain data in 51% of the nodes. That is the only way of making the network accept the change. Anything lower than 51% will make all nodes reject the update.

To effectively change a record in the Blockchain, you would have to modify the data in 25,001 nodes to make sure the network accepts your modifications. That would be the number assuming you have 50,000 nodes.

If you take into consideration that:

– Nodes are available all around the world

– People would have to give access to their computers and copies of the Bitcoin ledger

– Each person must agree with the change to alter the Blockchain

As you can see from the requirements, it is nearly impossible to make such type of change. The fact that each transaction is irreversible has both positive and negative aspects. It is a way to demonstrate trust because you know that you can't go back once you transfer Bitcoins to someone else. It also gives people trying to apply scams or fraud with Bitcoin the security of not getting a "chargeback."

2.6 Blockchain and security

From our description of the irreversibility nature of Bitcoin transactions, we can rest assured that transactions confirmed by the network are accurate. Aside from the multiple node confirmations, the network uses a lot of cryptography to ensure connections and transactions are free from hacking.

You get multiple levels of cryptography in the validation of transactions and also Bitcoin creation. The Blockchain software and Bitcoin network are secure and reliable. The only way of hacking the network is to gain control of the majority of nodes.

What about all those security problems and fraud involving Bitcoins? Most of those cases are using Bitcoin as a new form of scam, where an attacker tries to steal coins from a person with bad digital security habits.

Most of the attacks happen with web-based services that give you the convenience of managing the coins online. However, a security flaw can put your balance under the control of hackers and scammers. You give away the responsibility of managing your coins when using a web-based service.

If you start accumulating a significant balance in Bitcoins, you should never leave it in a web-based service. We will describe ways of secure your investment using a wide variety of methods.

The Blockchain and Bitcoin networks themselves are secure, and currently, there is no security issues or flaw in the network. If you want to start using Bitcoins, rest assured that the network is secure.

Tip: Most of the losses related to Bitcoin directly relate to exchange houses that facilitate the trading of Bitcoins and other cryptocurrencies. If you decide to buy cryptocurrency from an exchange, you should choose carefully and never leave the balance there for longer periods.

2.6.1 Blockchain bugs

Many people have a dream about opening their bank accounts and find that their account balances are multiplied by a huge number because of a software glitch. Wouldn't it be great to open the bank app and discover a few extra zeros? Like eight to ten extra zeros? That type of software glitch has a name of bug and is a common problem in computer systems.

Sadly, it is not common to find such types of problems in bank systems.

Do we have bugs in the Bitcoin network? Sure! Eventually, a group of people discovers a bug or problem in the network, and the community quickly deploys a fix to the software. Why the community? If you don't remember, the Bitcoin protocol is open-source.

In the history of Bitcoin, a bug is famous for allowing a person to generate 184 Billion Bitcoins. Yes, it is not a typo. Someone was able to create 184 Billion BTC. If you think about the hard limit of 21 Million BTC for the network, the hack represented a major problem.

A serious bug like this one was quickly spotted by a developer who found something strange in block 74638 from the Bitcoin ledger. After two hours, the core developers of Bitcoin started to fix the problem, and five hours later fixed it.

They even gave a name to the problem: "overflow bug."

Like any software or computer system, Bitcoin is not free of problems and issues caused by glitches in its code. Since it has a lot of attention and is open-source, the core developers can quickly spot problems and work on a fix. If they can't fix that quickly, anyone with knowledge of the code can contribute.

How do they fix the Blockchain? When something like that happens, the core developers might release a soft or hard fork of the Bitcoin software.

2.6.2 Bitcoin soft and hard forks

Like any software under heavy development, the Bitcoin core and Blockchain are not bug-free and eventually require fixes and new versions. At the moment, we have Bitcoin in version 0.20.1, and from time to time, it receives updates.

In the previous section, we described a bug that allowed someone to create an astronomical amount of Bitcoins. A "hacker" was able to create 184 Billion BTC with the famous "overflow bug." To fix the issue, the core developers released a soft fork of the network.

A fork is a type of derivate copy made from existing software. It is like making a full copy of the code and apply small changes.

For instance, we can compare a fork with something that you might do when attending a class. Imagine that you are attending a class and need to take notes to keep track of all lessons. You can start from scratch or use the notes from someone else as a starting point. By using other people's notes, you can avoid writing existing information and only add relevant observations. Both notes are very similar, with a few updates.

That is close to what we have in a soft fork. You make a copy and use most of the content with small changes.

A fork in the Blockchain might result in what we call a split. The split can result in nodes requiring an update to the Blockchain data or creating a different chain.

In the Bitcoin network, we eventually have soft and hard forks:

– **Soft fork:** Usually, a soft fork enforce rules and small changes to the Blockchain data. The resulting data is backward compatible.

– **Hard fork:** Here, we add new rules and features to the Blockchain. As a result, all data is not backward compatible. It usually means you have a different type of Blockchain.

A popular hard fork of the Bitcoin network is Bitcoin cash. At the time, many developers tried to make changes to the protocol to enable faster transaction confirmation. The community rejected the idea, and from that point, they created a hard fork of Bitcoin. That is a separate Blockchain with unique rules.

2.6.3 The double-spending problem

A digital currency like Bitcoin has a common problem they must address to increase all transactions' reliability, which is double-spending. What is double-spending, and why should you care about it? We can start by describing the problem and how it is not an issue with traditional payment methods.

Imagine that you have a 20 Dollar bill and decide to put some gas into your car. You go to the gas station and spend the money. On your way out, you enter a grocery store. There you won't be able to spend that same 20 Dollar bill. You already used it in the gas station. It is hard to double-spend the same money once it leaves your pocket.

What about digital money? If you have that same amount as the balance of your bank account, it will be up to the bank system to avoid double-spending. For instance, if you go to the gas station and spend 20 dollars in gas using your debit card. The bank system verifies that you have enough balance to pay and authorizes the transaction.

After you leave the gas station and tries to use the same twenty dollars with groceries, the bank system probably won't approve the transaction. It checks your account and sees that you don't have that money anymore. They are responsible for avoiding double-spending.

What about Bitcoins? Can you double-spend with Bitcoins? The Blockchain also handles the double-spending of cryptocurrencies. It works based on the number of confirmations from nodes. For instance, if you have 1 BTC and tries to send that same amount to two different people. We can call them transactions A and B.

Once you start transaction A, the network gives you the first confirmation, and right after that, you also get a confirmation for transaction B.

The second confirmation for transaction A triggers the network to reject all other transaction B checks. It identifies the same amount with ongoing confirmations and fails to confirm any more changes to transaction B.

The network identifies that a certain amount is in use for another transaction and will not confirm the change. Having a credit card declined when trying to make a purchase if you don't have a credit limit anymore. For that reason, most people wait for about four to six confirmations from the network to ensure a transaction is valid. After that number of confirmations, it is safe to assume that it is a valid transaction.

That is how Bitcoin deals with double-spending. Any attempt to send the same amount makes the network reject the transaction.

2.7 Blockchain limitations

After you start managing Bitcoins, you can quickly wonder why retail stores don't widely accept the currency? It is a safe and reliable way of adding another way of payment to your customers. If you look online, you can find a shortlist with retail stores that accept Bitcoin as a way of payment for goods and services.

What is the problem of taking Bitcoins as a way of payment? Two main issues keep retail stores away from accepting Bitcoins:

– Price fluctuations

– Network speed

The network speed is an issue when you think about the required number of confirmations to consider a transaction secure. Depending on the network congestion, you might have to wait from 10 to 60 minutes to get all those six confirmations.

Imagine going to the grocery store after having to wait for 20 minutes until you have a confirmation for your payment. As a result, you probably would have huge lines of people waiting to confirm their payments.

It doesn't get easier when you think about the price fluctuations. The first problem is that some costs of a business don't accept Bitcoin payments like taxes. The business also has to pay salaries and cover costs like rent. If Bitcoin prices go up, you are good to go, but it could mean a high-risk to the business if they drop a lot.

That is a huge limitation for the widespread adoption of Bitcoin as a payment method in everyday purchases. I know some retailers accept cryptocurrency as a payment method, but they are still hard to find.

Other cryptocurrencies like Ether offers better transaction confirmation speeds and are an alternative to Bitcoin.

What is next?

Blockchain is by far one of the most promising technologies today and has the potential to disrupt many established fields and tasks. You know, have a great understanding of how Bitcoin works and the coin relation to the Blockchain.

To educate yourself even more and explore the Blockchain, you can start to look at the tools provided in the chapter that gives you access to Blockchain data. For instance, look at transactions and how they happen in a matter of minutes or hours.

If you find a website that offers Bitcoin donations, you can quickly take the donation address and check how many coins the owner of the address received. It is a great exercise to learn more about Blockchain transactions and give you an overview of the network.

Our next natural step is to start preparing to create a wallet and interact with the Blockchain. That is our goal in the next chapter!

Chapter 3 - The Bitcoin wallet

It is time to start playing with your first cryptocurrency wallet to receive and send Bitcoins! Before jumping into a wallet, we have to define some crucial aspects of the cryptocurrency wallet, like the pair of keys used to manage and control the balance.

The entire chapter explains how they work and the benefits and liabilities of the system. You probably heard that with Bitcoin, you can become a bank, which is true, but it also brings security responsibility. You must know the risks and avoid future problems.

Here is a list of what you will learn in this chapter:

– How the cryptocurrency wallet works

– Relation between Bitcoins and a wallet

– How the Public and Private Keys works

– Is Bitcoin a messaging system?

– Creating your first wallet

– Why not use Bitcoin Core as your wallet?

– When to use multiple wallets

3.1 Understanding the digital wallet

At this point, you know a lot about how the Blockchain works and the workflow behind the technology. The next step is to start handling and using a digital wallet. The name wallet is familiar to most of us because very early on in our lives when you begin to receive money from your parents, they probably gifted you with a wallet.

You can get a cheap or expensive design worth hundreds of dollars, but they all have the same purpose: to hold your money in a comfortable location.

Today we also have digital wallets that can help you with transactions and electronic money on your computer, phone, or smartwatch. Some of the most popular digital wallet options include:

– Apple Pay

– Google Pay

– PayPal

Those wallets can work with contactless technology in your phone and store credit and debit card numbers to secure transactions. If you used any one of those wallets to pay for services or products, you have a great idea of how those types of digital payment systems work.

When Satoshi Nakamoto proposed Bitcoin, he introduced a wallet concept, which we use today to manage and move the digital coin between people and institutions. The handling of your digital wallet is the most important aspect of Bitcoin management. Depending on the type of wallet and security measurements, you can make it vulnerable to loss and theft or "bulletproof."

If you do a quick search for a Bitcoin wallet, you will find dozens of options available. It is crucial to choose wisely where you will manage the cryptocurrency. Why are there so many options regarding wallets? The Bitcoin protocol is open-source, and anyone can design and create software wallets that with the Blockchain.

If you think about traditional money, you also have the same types of problems regarding storing cash. For instance, imagine that you received an inheritance of one million dollars in bills of 100 and 50. That is a lot of money to hold and store. What is the best way to keep this money safe?

Most of us will probably deposit the money in a bank because you transfer to the bank to secure it. What if you don't trust the bank? In case you want to keep the money nearby, there are multiple options:

– Buy a safe and keep it in your house

– Hide the cash with no safe in your home. Maybe a suitcase in a closet?

– Go to a remote location and bury it in the ground (please make a map to locate it later)

All those options are valid alternatives to store the money received from the inheritance. However, they all present potential risks. The first one is the theft of your money as soon word spread that you keep that much cash in the house. You will most likely become a target.

In case you want to play treasure hunt and bury the money in the ground, you could forget the exact location where you placed it or lose the instructions to help you find it later. Or even worse, someone else could find it first!

When choosing a wallet to manage your Bitcoins or any other cryptocurrency, you must evaluate all benefits and possible issues. This will help you avoid security risks and the potential loss of your digital coins.

3.1.1 Bitcoins and the wallet

One question that many beginners might ask themselves; where do you save the Bitcoins? Can you open them as text files? Is it a file on your computer? After explaining how the Blockchain works, it will be easier to understand the relation between a wallet and digital coins.

First of all, we can start by making it clear that you don't store Bitcoins locally. All the Bitcoins are part of the Blockchain ledger. When you create a wallet, the coin balance goes to that wallet address.

A common misconception about Bitcoin is that all your coins will be inside the device or software when you create a wallet. That is not the truth. A cryptocurrency wallet works like your username and password for a bank app. You can install the app on your phone and manage the funds with the login credentials. But, no digital cash is on the phone. If you lose the phone, you can get a new one and restore your access with the same credentials.

The same principle applies to Bitcoin. You don't keep any kind of digital data related to Bitcoins locally. Your wallet has the credentials to manage and control the Bitcoin balance. All coins are part of the Blockchain ledger.

When you want to send coins to someone else, you must:

– Use the credentials to access the balance (Private key)

– Insert the wallet recipient address (Public key)

– Set the desired amount of coins you want to send

If you submit this transaction, the network checks the available balance of your wallet, and if you have enough funds, it will confirm the transaction. Based on the Bitcoin ledger, a node must verify if you control the funds. Once they verify your credentials are valid and have funds, it considers the transaction as accurate. The balance of both wallets receives an update based on the transfer.

Info: *What happens when you give your bank credentials to someone else? You will be at risk of losing all the funds. The same applies to your Bitcoin wallet. You should never disclose the Private Keys to anyone other than yourself!*

3.1.2 Public address and Private keys

The Bitcoin wallet is the most important part of any person's strategy to hold and safeguard cryptocurrency. What is a wallet? In the cryptocurrency world, a wallet is a collection of two fundamental pieces of information:

– **Public key**: The address used to receive deposits

– **Private key**: The code that gives you control over a wallet balance

To better understand what those two keys are, we can compare a Bitcoin wallet to another technology that I believe you are familiar. They work in a similar way to an e-mail provider.

Imagine that you have an e-mail account to send and receive electronic messages. You have multiple options to register for an e-mail account, like free providers such as Gmail and Yahoo, or go with a hosting company.

When thinking about an e-mail account, we can describe it with three essential parts:

- **Address**: The public address of your e-mail could be *yourname@somedomain.com*.

- **Password**: To manage and send messages from your domain, you usually need to set a password to ensure only you have access.

- **Messages**: The messages you receive are held in a remote computer, in the "cloud," and with the login credentials, you can access the account to manage and send messages to other addresses.

That is a system we use every day for quite some time, and you are probably familiar with all the terms and workflow. When comparing an e-mail system to Bitcoin, we can easily associate:

- E-mail address = Public key

- Password = Private key

- E-mail messages = Bitcoins

When you have to receive a message from someone else, give them the e-mail address. You can safely disclose the address to anyone because they can't do anything without the password. We never share our e-mail passwords with anyone.

The same applies to the Bitcoin wallet and all cryptocurrencies, where you can securely give the Public key or address to receive deposits. Your Private Key is the most critical part of a digital wallet holding Bitcoins. If a third party has access to the Private Key, you will most likely lose your Bitcoins.

Info: Most of the scams involving Bitcoins and cryptocurrencies tries to make a person give away their Private Keys. With the possession of this information, anyone can restore a wallet and transfer the funds. It is something you must take seriously!

As we mentioned in previous chapters, the Bitcoin protocol uses cryptography to ensure you have a secure environment. The Public and Private keys work in pairs to encrypt and decrypt information. Some people usually say that Bitcoin is a secure messaging system because of that analogy with an e-mail account. The Public and Private keys work as a way to encrypt and decrypt those messages.

What happens if you lose or forget the Private Key? It is simple; you lose access to the balance in your wallet. The Bitcoins are lost forever. Can you call anyone for help? No, there is no one you can call for help or assistance. It is your sole responsibility to keep that information secure.

For that reason, it is a wise idea to pick a wallet that offers a way to backup your data. There are options with backup systems involving a mnemonic Phrase or seed. Most of the software-based wallets use this method. It is easier to remind of a series of random words than a complex code.

How complex is a Private Key? A Private Key in a Bitcoin wallet is a 256-Bit number with a random nature and spawns as soon you create the wallet. Here is an example of a Private Key:

– L2ck4a55B7kXjtePBjYuJupo000jKwsem1a0000WL2DHe5B000

You need this type of code to send Bitcoins from a wallet as a validator for the Blockchain. It should remain a secret and hold in a safe location. A compressed Private Key will start with either an "L" or "K." The uncompressed format starts with a "5".

What about the Public key? During the wallet generation process, the first information created is the Private Key. Based on complex math operations, it generates a Public Key. The Public Address looks like this:

– 1MZ4000Qe000LE00H0fL7e100h2sxNbDR

It always starts with a "1," and it is the address you can safely share with anyone to receive Bitcoins. There are other formats of Public Keys available that starts with a "bc1" or "3":

– **Starting with 1:** Legacy Public Key

– **Starting with 3:** P2SH Public Key

– **Starting with bc1:** SEGWIT Public Key

Those are all different protocols for wallets and works in a similar way. Today, most software wallets use Public Keys with the SEGWIT protocol to generate smaller transaction data and save money on fees. Later in the book, we will discuss more about fees.

An interesting aspect of those keys is that you don't need an internet connection to create the pair. They share a mathematical relation, and the Blockchain recognizes them based on that math. You can create as many addresses as you like. A Public Key only goes to the Bitcoin ledger if it receives funds. Otherwise, there is no need to keep a record of that address.

How to create a pair of keys? The workflow to create a wallet with those keys is:

1. Create a Private Key

2. From the Private Key, generate a Public Key

3. Get a public address

Do you have to do any math to generate those addresses? No, your wallet does the work for you. All the process happens based on heavy cryptography and math. Can we reverse the workflow and get the Private Key from a Public Address? It is technically possible with enough time and a powerful computer.

How much time? Assuming you have a powerful computer, like a supercomputer, an estimate to guess the possible 2^{256} possible combinations for a Private Key would require about 600 million years. This is for one single Private Key. As soon you spend the Bitcoins before that period, your balance should be safe.

A possible threat to Bitcoin security is quantum computers that are multiple times more powerful than existing computers. With a quantum computer, a person could break the security of a Private Key in a matter of seconds! How close are we to those computers? At least a few decades or centuries. That is assuming the Bitcoin code doesn't receive an update to adapt to those computers.

Info: As mentioned before, all keys shared in this chapter are not valid for network transitions.

3.1.3 Bitcoin is a messaging system

Whenever you think about Bitcoin or cryptocurrencies, what is the first thing coming to your mind? It is a digital currency that is revolutionary and is changing the way we relate to money. It is probably what many people think about the digital coin.

What if I told you that Bitcoin is a messaging system? A secure messaging system.

In the Bitcoin network, a transaction is a message that needs a digital signature for validation. This validation comes from the use of a Private Key that matches the Public Key. What happens if they don't match? The network rejects such transactions.

A digital signature created by the combination of Private and Public keys depends on several factors, and you can't emulate or fake it. That is part of the cryptography behind all the process and makes the messaging system incredibly secure.

Info: When using a software wallet or a tool to help you manage the Bitcoins, you probably won't have to deal with a Private Key in its "pure" state. The software will most likely offer you a way of using something like a pass Phrase to avoid the need of handling a Private Key.

3.1.4 Creating your first wallet

How hard is it to create a Bitcoin wallet with a Public and Private key? The process of making a wallet is simple, and you can do that using software. A popular option in the Bitcoin ecosystem to quickly create a wallet is the useful bitaddress.org website.

The system is a port of the code responsible for creating Private and Public keys that work in a website. You can visit:

```
https://www.bitaddresss.org
```

There you will find multiple options to make the first wallet. To keep it truly a random process, the site interface asks for user input to generate the Private Key (Figure 3.1).

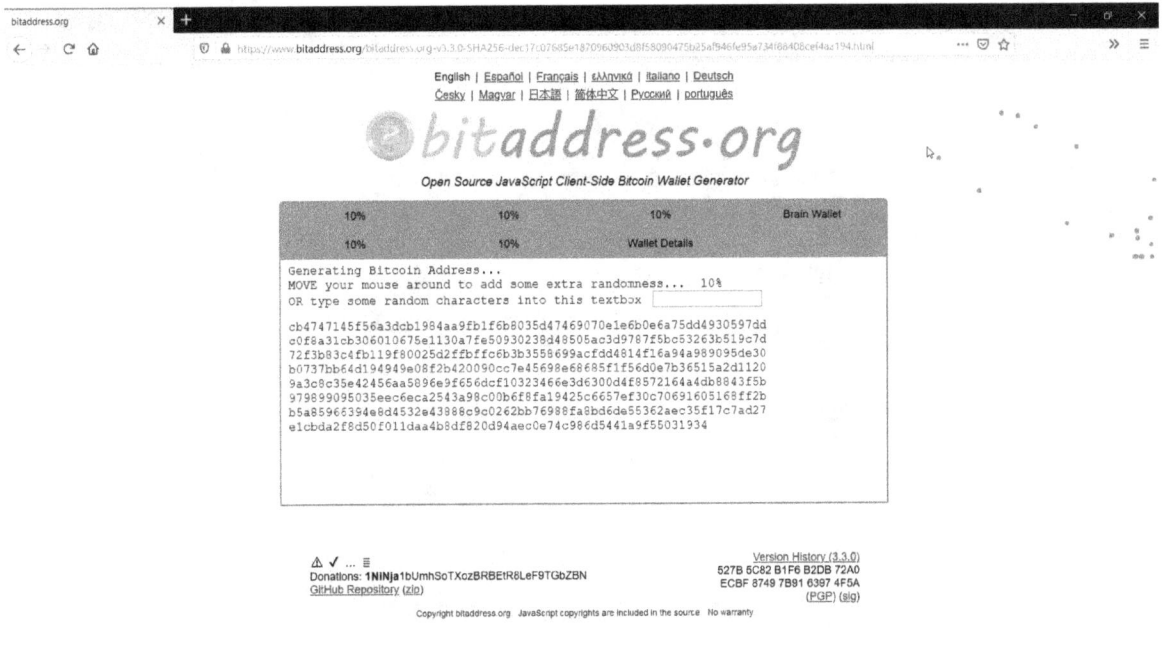

Figure 3.1 - Bitaddress

You can either move the mouse cursor to random locations and directions or type letters and numbers in the text box. The small green dots on the screen are mouse cursor locations captured by the system.

You will see a progress bar showing how much more input you need to get the Private Key. Once you reach 100%, you will see the Private and Public keys for your first address (Figure 3.2).

Figure 3.2 - First address

As you can see from the results, you have both Private and Public Keys. You could start to send Bitcoins to that Public address immediately. However, I strongly advise you not to use this address just yet. That is not because the process of bitaddress.org has a security flaw, but because your computer might have a security issue like malware scanning for Private Keys.

Later in the chapter, we will discuss the risks of generating Private keys in a compromised computer.

Info: Parts of Figure 3.2 received a blur effect to hide the addresses and QR Codes.

3.1.5 Offline wallet creation

A bank account is what we use to manage money and keep track of investments and savings in our daily financial operations. Usually, you receive an account and routing number as your unique credentials. Besides that, you also need a PIN to make transactions with your debit card.

To open that account, you have to contact the bank and provide documents to check your identity and, eventually, proof of income to receive benefits.

Unlike a traditional bank that requires an initial deposit and identification to open an account, you can create as many Bitcoin wallets as you want. An ingenious aspect of wallet creation is that you can make them offline with no internet connection.

Both the Private and Public keys have a mathematical relation that can receive validation using the Bitcoin network's cryptography calculations. Since the Blockchain only registers transactions between wallets, an address with zero transactions doesn't need to a record in the Bitcoin ledger.

For that reason, you can create as many wallets as you want using off-line software.

An incredibly secure way of making a "bulletproof" wallet is to use a computer that never went online with a clean install of a browser and operating system. That is what lots of experienced Bitcoin users do when they want to create an offline wallet or cold wallet.

How does it work? If you look at the bottom of the bitaddresss.org website, you will see a link to download the wallet generator's source code (Figure 3.3).

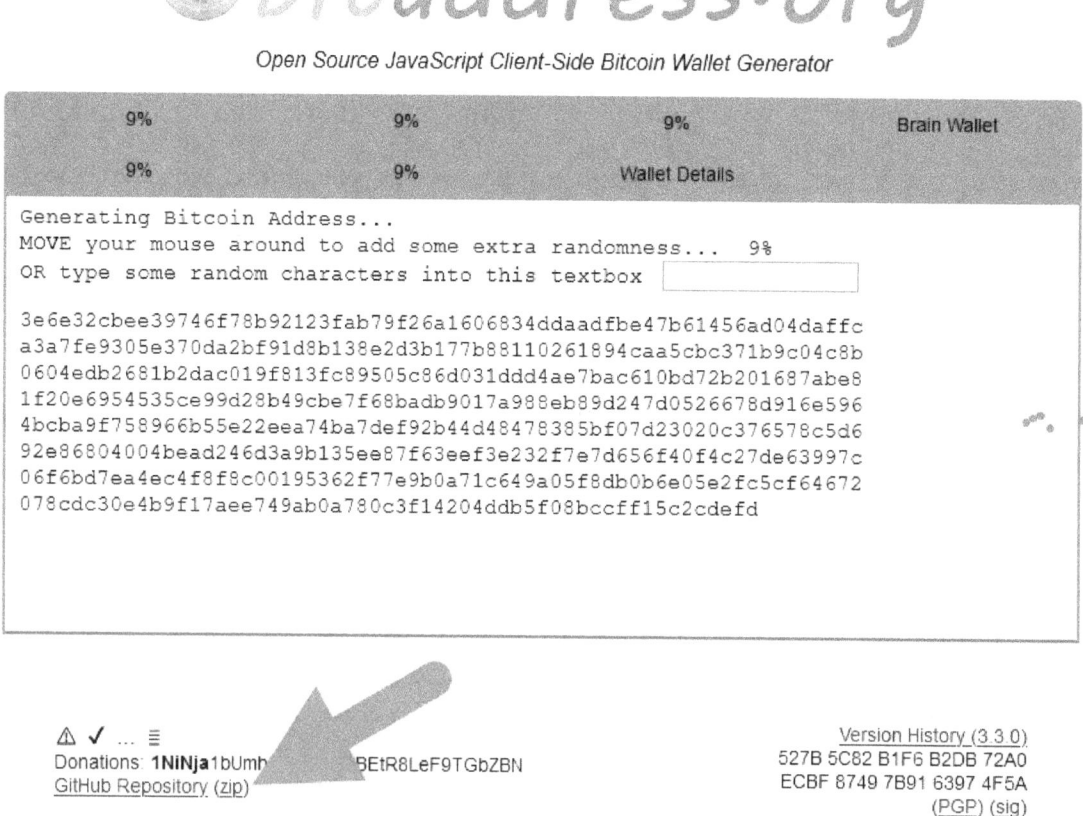

Figure 3.3 - *Code download*

You can open the file with an HTML extension after extracting the ZIP contents and open that in your browser. It will work the same way as a local process. However, like mentioned before, you can only guarantee the Private Key security when using a system that has never been connected to the internet.

Here is what some people do to create secure wallets:

1. Download a bootable version of a Linux system like Ubuntu and save it to a USB flash drive (https://ubuntu.com/tutorials/create-a-usb-stick-on-windows)

2. Copy the contents of the source from bitaddress.org to another Flash Drive

3. Disconnect your computer from the network

4. Boot the computer using the Linux USB drive

5. Open Firefox or Chrome after entering the Linux system

6. Open the bit address.org source and create a wallet

7. Direct connect a printer to the computer using a USB cable

8. Print the wallet information

Assuming you didn't make any digital copies of the wallet information in either plain text or PDF, the only location where your wallet data exists is the sheet of paper out of your printer. The printed paper is now your wallet.

The Private and Public Key exists only on that piece of paper! Of course, you have another type of security liability with this system. If you lose the paper, you also lose access to the balance in that wallet.

Info: *The method describe a way of having a paper wallet that is secure because it keeps the most sensitive information out from your computer, which is the Private Key. No one can hack a piece of paper.*

3.1.6 Should I use Bitcoin core?

In a previous chapter, we mentioned a Bitcoin client's existence that you could download and install on any computer called Bitcoin core. It will give you a way of participating in the Bitcoin network, and it also offers a wallet to keep your coins.

Should you download it and use it as a wallet? The short answer is; no.

Unless you want to take part in the Bitcoin network to validate and have a local copy of the Blockchain file in your computer, you have much easier wallet options.

If you decide to use it anyway, you should know that it requires downloading the entire Blockchain ledger, which is close to a 320GB download at the moment (Figure 3.4).

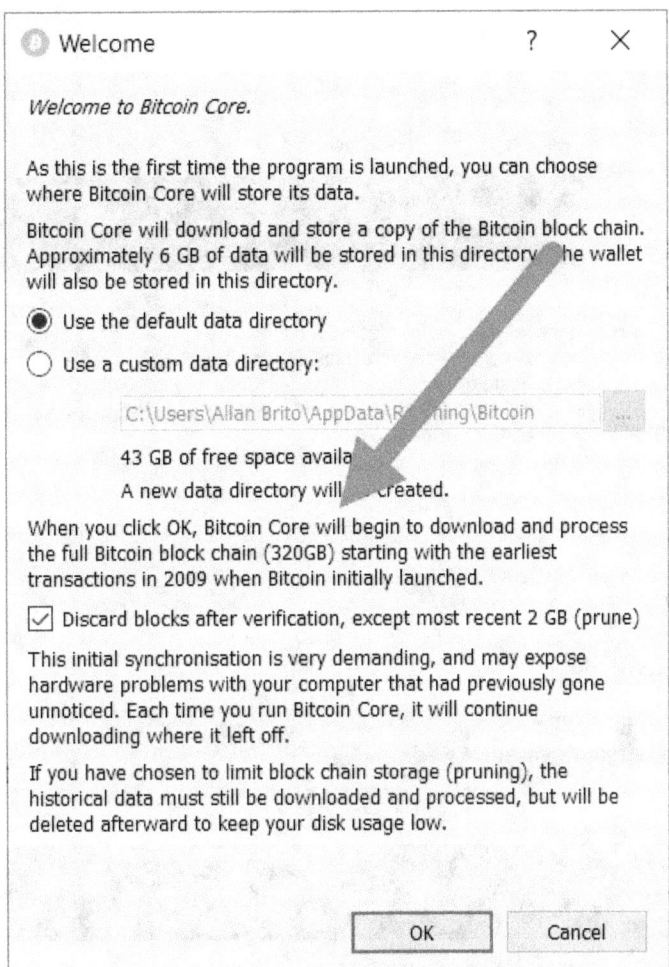

Figure 3.4 - Setup screen from Bitcoin core

It downloads all blocks progressively, with transactions dating back to 2009. All downloaded data needs verification and will consume a lot of resources from your computer.

In my case, it was giving an estimate of 26 weeks of processing to join the network. In the Bitcoin core, you can easily create a Wallet from the File menu.

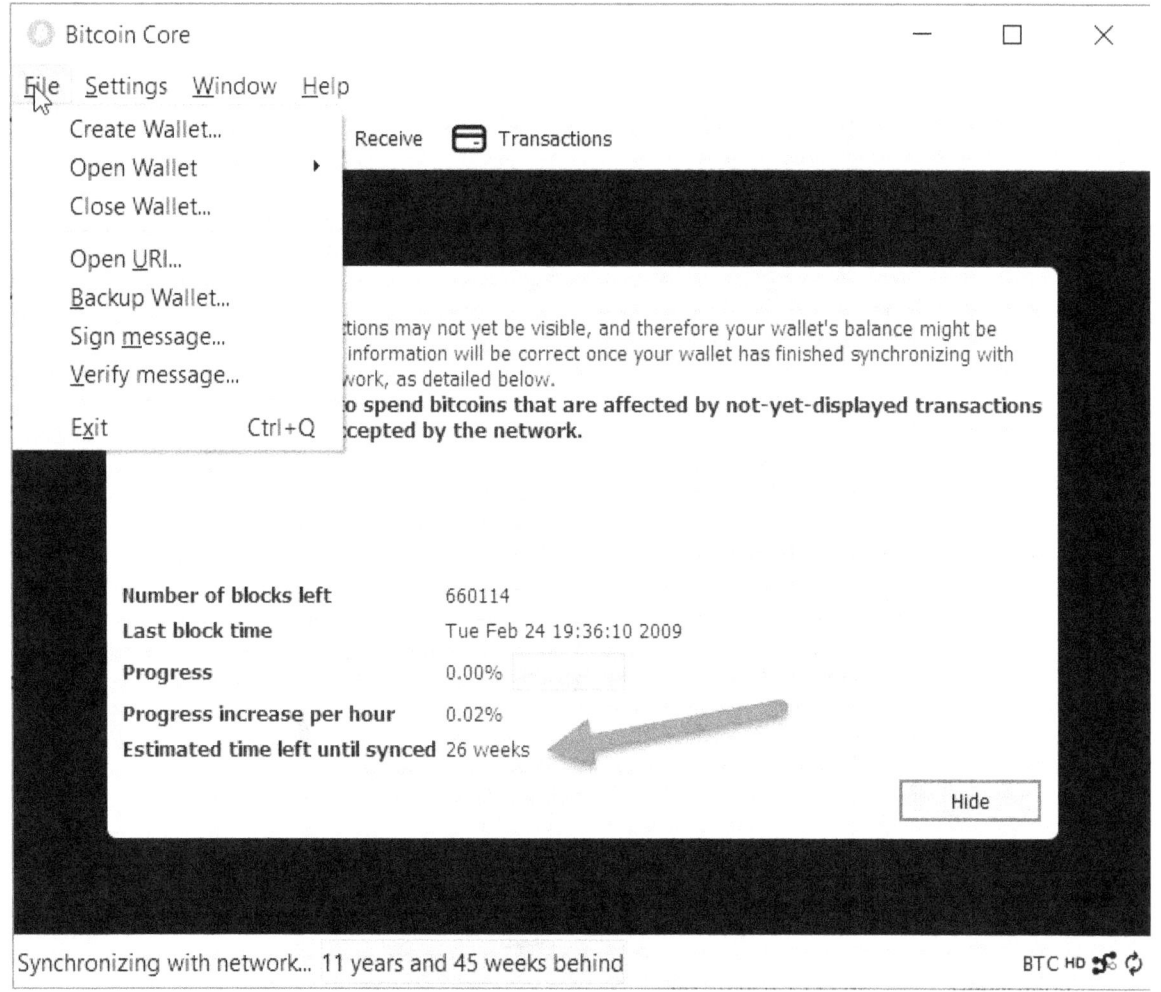

Figure 3.5 - The processing time and Wallet creation

It is possible to assign a name to the Wallet and start sending and receiving Bitcoins from there (Figure 3.6).

Figure 3.6 - Bitcoin Core Wallet

You can visit bitcoin.org and download the Bitcoin Core for your computer.

The best options for beginners are wallets that don't take part in the network and give you extra features to secure the Private Key with backup options.

3.1.7 Checking a wallet balance

The Blockchain and all Bitcoin ledger are open to anyone to join and retrieve information from all transactions. As a result, you can easily check the balance of any Bitcoin wallet. The only thing you need is the Public Key. You can even check the balance of a newly created wallet with no funds.

An easy way of doing that is with the help of online systems like:

https://www.blockchain.com/en/explorer

https://blockchair.com/

https://btc.com/

Any of those sites give us detailed information about Bitcoin exchange rates and let us search for a transaction and check the balance of a wallet by entering the Public Key. We already mentioned this "feature" of the Blockchain, but you can expand that even further with your addresses.

Start checking for Wallet balances! For instance, you can check the wallet used to receive donations to the Bitcoin Foundation (bitcoin.org). At their site, you find an address where anyone can send donations:

```
3E8ociqZa9mZUSwGdSmAEMAoAxBK3FNDcd
```

How much they have in this wallet? At the moment, after checking their transaction history, they have 0.06166728 BTC in their balance. Across the years, they received a total of 12.04603381 BTC.

Considering today's exchange rates, it is equivalent to:

– 2,000 USD (balance)

– 400,000 USD (received)

You can do the same with any wallet address you have. Why do they have a small value in their balance? Usually, we have a wallet to receive transfers, but it is usually not the same wallet used to save the coins. For instance, you can send coins to a wallet in an exchange to trade for fiat currency.

Another interesting exercise is to check some of the most valuable wallets in the Blockchain. Like we mentioned before, even if you are a Bitcoin millionaire, you can't hide the wallet balance. Everyone can see and check the Public Key, but they won't link that to a person or entity.

You can even find online lists with the most valuable wallets from the Bitcoin ledger:

`https://99bitcoins.com/bitcoin/rich-list/`

The wallet with the highest receiving transaction history is:

After checking this wallet's balance, you will find out that it has an impressive received amount of 297347.11745676 BTC. That is equivalent to 10,003,556,894.99 USD. Based on multiple user reports and a widely used address, the wallet is probably from an exchange called Binance.

Info: What happens when you create a wallet with no transactions and try to retrieve their balance? If that is a valid Public Key, you will get a balance of 0 BTC as a result.

3.2 Using multiple wallets

As you will soon realize after starting to use and trade Bitcoins or any other cryptocurrency, a wallet is a critical aspect of any strategy to keep coins in a safe location. We can use a hypothetical situation where you have to manage a large amount of money.

If you had a bank account with a large balance, like 5 million dollars, would you leave it sitting in a single bank? To make it harder for you to lose that money if the account becomes compromised, it is wise to split it into multiple accounts and even banks.

One account with a balance for your daily needs and others for long term investment or savings. That way, in case you have a problem like a bank going out of business or someone, hacks the PIN from one of the accounts, you will have to re-cover only part of the money.

The same concept applies to Bitcoins and cryptocurrencies. Since you can easily create multiple wallets at no cost, it is easy to manage and split the balance in multiple addresses. Why is that a good idea? As mentioned before, the most important and critical part of any wallet is the Private Key. If you lose this information or somehow got hacked, you lose the balance of a wallet.

Info: Remember that a wallet doesn't hold any Bitcoin data. It has Private and Public Keys. All Bitcoins remain safe in the Blockchain.

After the coins leave the wallet, the process is irreversible once it goes to the ledger. A hacker or scammer can take your Bitcoins knowing that it is irreversible.

Later we will discuss the use of exchanges to buy Bitcoins. A common strategy is to create a wallet where you want to keep coins for long periods. After buying coins from the exchange, you can quickly transfer them to this wallet.

It will work as a "deposit" wallet that only receives transfers from coins purchased from exchanges. As it mainly receives deposits, you never have to type or use the Private Key, which reduces a hack's risk.

3.2.1 Saving your Private Keys

Those long term wallets face another type of challenge. The storage and retrieval of your Private Keys. How to keep them safe?

For instance, imagine that you had to create an email account back in 2012. That email account has a strong password with 30 characters, including digits and symbols. If you have to open this email account today after all those years, would you remember the password?

For most people, the answer would be no. A password used for the last time 10 years ago? You probably will use the recovery options from the account to change the password to something else.

Depending on the type of wallet you choose to manage your Bitcoins, you don't have that option to recover a lost Private Key. If you don't keep it in a safe location that only you can easily access, you probably will lose access to your coins.

Tip: Having the Private Keys in a computer is always a risk, but if you decide to use software to keep track of them, it is important to ensure it is safe. There are lots of password managers today offering safe locations to keep your data. However, it would be better to keep this information out of your computer.

What is next?

After this chapter, you probably became scared about the possibility of losing the Private Keys, and it is always a risk, and have a Bitcoin balance you can't use. There are multiple cases of people with locked balances in accounts with a few or thousands of Bitcoins.

If you don't want to join them and have the balances locked, you should start from day one to find a way to secure the Private Keys.

The next natural step in your path to use Bitcoin is to pick a wallet and start managing a balance. In the next chapter, we will discuss multiple options and alternatives regarding wallets and which ones you should use.

Chapter 4 - How to choose a wallet?

As soon you start to search for a cryptocurrency wallet, you realize that you have hundreds of options. What is the best solution regarding a wallet to manage and keep your precious coins? In the following chapter, you will learn the benefits and risks of using multiple types of wallets.

Starting with both desktop and mobile wallets' setup process to the benefits of adopting a hardware device to store all your sensitive information inside. You also find a new information type data that you must keep save, your recovery phrase.

That collection of random words replaces the need to backup your Private Keys and get back your funds if something goes wrong with the wallet.

Here is a list of what you will learn:

– How to choose and types of wallets

– How to use mnemonic phrases to recover a wallet?

– Using Desktop wallets

– Using Mobile wallets

– Using Web-based wallets

– Using hardware wallets

4.1 Types of wallets

The cryptocurrency wallet is a critical element to manage digital coins, and unlike many people think it doesn't hold any coins. Instead, It works as an interface to communicate and send transactions to the Bitcoin ledger. I will never get tired to repeat that you should always protect and ensure you don't lose the wallet's Private Keys.

Since you don't keep Bitcoins in the wallet, the Private Keys are the only thing in your possession.

4.1.1 Choosing a wallet

It is time to pick a wallet and start holding and trading Bitcoins. What is the best type of wallet? In the early days, we mainly had the Bitcoin Core Wallet as the single option to interact with the Blockchain. After a while, we started to see more additional options regarding wallets.

There are multiple types of wallets with features and unique tools to help you make easier transactions, protect your balance, and conceal the Private Keys. Some of the best wallets manage the Private Keys so that not even you can see them, which reduces the risk of a possible compromise. Instead of managing the keys directly, you can use a Recovery Phrase or a PIN.

Before picking a wallet to hold your valuable coins, it is important to understand how they work and all the benefits and risks from each one of them.

Regarding Bitcoin and cryptocurrency wallets, we can start by separating them into two large groups:

– Hot wallets

– Cold wallets

The designation of a Hot or Cold wallet directly relates to how it connects to the internet. With a Hot wallet, you have an interface to the Blockchain that is in constant connection to the web. That is convenient to make quick transactions and use in exchanges.

On the other hand, we have the Cold wallets that are an offline device that has your Private Keys. This type of device usually goes online only when you have to make a transaction and is one of the most secure ways to protect your Private Keys. A piece of paper is a great example of a Cold Wallet. You can't hack a paper.

You will find multiple examples of both Cold and Hot wallets during your time managing and investing in cryptocurrencies. It is inevitable to use both types eventually.

From these two main categories, regarding connectivity, we can also use five big categories of wallet types:

– Desktop wallets (Hot)

– Mobile wallets (Hot)

– Web-based wallets (Burning Hot)

– Hardware wallets (Cold)

– Paper wallets (Cold)

Some people also use a three-type classification: desktop, mobile, and web-based as software wallets.

Each one of those wallets offers benefits and also potential risks to hold and trade cryptocurrencies. Notice that I placed a reference for Hot or Cold wallets. The Web-based wallet is burning hot because it is the most dangerous type with a history of security breaches.

You can use any one of them to hold cryptocurrencies, but some are better for quick transactions, and others become invaluable tools for secure and long term deposits.

If you want to check for recommendations from the Bitcoin Foundation regarding wallets, they have an interesting page with multiple options and a feature comparison:

```
https://bitcoin.org/en/choose-your-wallet
```

There you also find links to download and more information regarding each wallet type.

4.2 Private Keys and Mnemonic Phrase

You already know the importance of your Private Keys in a wallet at this point in the book. If you think it is a minor problem, you can do a quick search on forums like Reddit, or Google the subject, to see terrible histories about people who lost their coins by mishandling Private Keys.

I recently found a history about a person who lost almost 3 BTC from a wallet because he failed to back up from a Desktop wallet. He was transferring data from an old computer to a new device. After getting the new computer files, the wallet software asked for his recovery phrase, which encrypts the Private Key.

He couldn't find any reference to the recovery phrase in his records, including a password manager and printed documents. As a result, he was locked out of the wallet and could not sign transfers. His balance is available in the Bitcoin Blockchain, but he can't move it anywhere. It is around 100,000 USD lost forever.

Most wallets that offer backup or recovery of data give you a mnemonic or recovery phrase upon setup. The software can generate the Private Key based on the recovery phrase. How is that phrase?

Most of the time is a sequence of 12 or 24 random words. The wallet gives you the words in a sequence, and you must take note of each word. To make it work, you have to remember the exact order.

Here is an example of a recovery phrase:

1. blue

2. square

3. blue

4. yes

5. modify

6. space

7. aspect

8. billing

9. sandwich

10. airplane

11. woman

12. six

Does this phrase make sense? No, but it is a random sequence of words that is nearly impossible to guess. When you set up a software wallet, it usually shows this phrase only once, and you have to find a way to save it. Writing on paper is the best solution.

That also prevents you from using the long and hard to memorize Private Key.

Use a password manager or write them down on paper. Regardless of the method, you need a reliable system to recover the data. If you want to move the wallet data from a computer to a new device, using the recovery phrase will give you back access to all Private Keys in a wallet.

Tip: You can even use the recovery phrase to keep synced versions of a wallet on both Desktop and mobile. Using the same phrase gives access to the same Private Keys.

4.3 Desktop wallets

A great way to start managing your cryptocurrencies is with a Desktop wallet. They receive this name because those wallets are computer programs that you must download and install on your computer.

Most of those wallets offer versions for multiple systems like:

– Windows

– macOS

– Linux

We already covered a type of Desktop wallet! The Bitcoin Core is a wallet that works on a computer. However, we still think it is not the best option for beginners and even advanced users looking to trade and keep coins in the long term.

What other options do we recommend for a Desktop wallet? Here are a few of my personal choices:

– Exodus (https://www.exodus.io)

– Electrum (https://electrum.org)

– Atomic Wallet (https://atomicwallet.io)

Unlike the Bitcoin Core that is a full node wallet and requires a copy of the Blockchain, all those wallets above are SPV wallets. The SPV means *Simplified Payment Verification* and represents a lightweight type of wallet that can interact with the Bitcoin Blockchain but doesn't require a full copy of their data.

It makes the process a lot easier!

Info: Another benefit of those wallets is that they support Bitcoin and dozens of other cryptocurrencies. The Bitcoin Core only works with Bitcoins.

From a beginner point of view, the best option with a friendly user-interface and resources is by far Exodus. I also like a lot the Atomic Wallet, with a great interface and resources.

You can use either of them to start with a Desktop wallet. The Atomic Wallet gains extra points for being open-source, ensuring that nothing strange is happening under the hood. When dealing with cryptocurrencies, you should always prefer *open-source* tools. It makes verification and auditing by developers easy to find potential security risks.

Info: All those Desktop wallets are decentralized, non-custodial options. It means the Private Keys and information stays in your device.

4.3.1 How to set up a desktop wallet?

To give you an example of how a Desktop wallet works, we can start the setup process to install Atomic Wallet. Each different wallet might give you unique steps and requirements, but they all share similar tools. Like mentioned before, I picked Atomic Wallet because it is open-source. But, it doesn't mean other wallets are bad, or you should not use them.

The first step to start with Atomic Wallet is to visit their website and download the appropriate installer for your system. In my case, I will use the Windows 10 version. You can also use the wallet in macOS and Linux.

Info: Always double check to see if you visit the correct website before downloading wallet software.

After downloading the file and installing it on your computer, you can open the Atomic Wallet app to begin the setup process. In the first screen, you will see an option to create a new wallet or restore it from a backup (Figure 4.1).

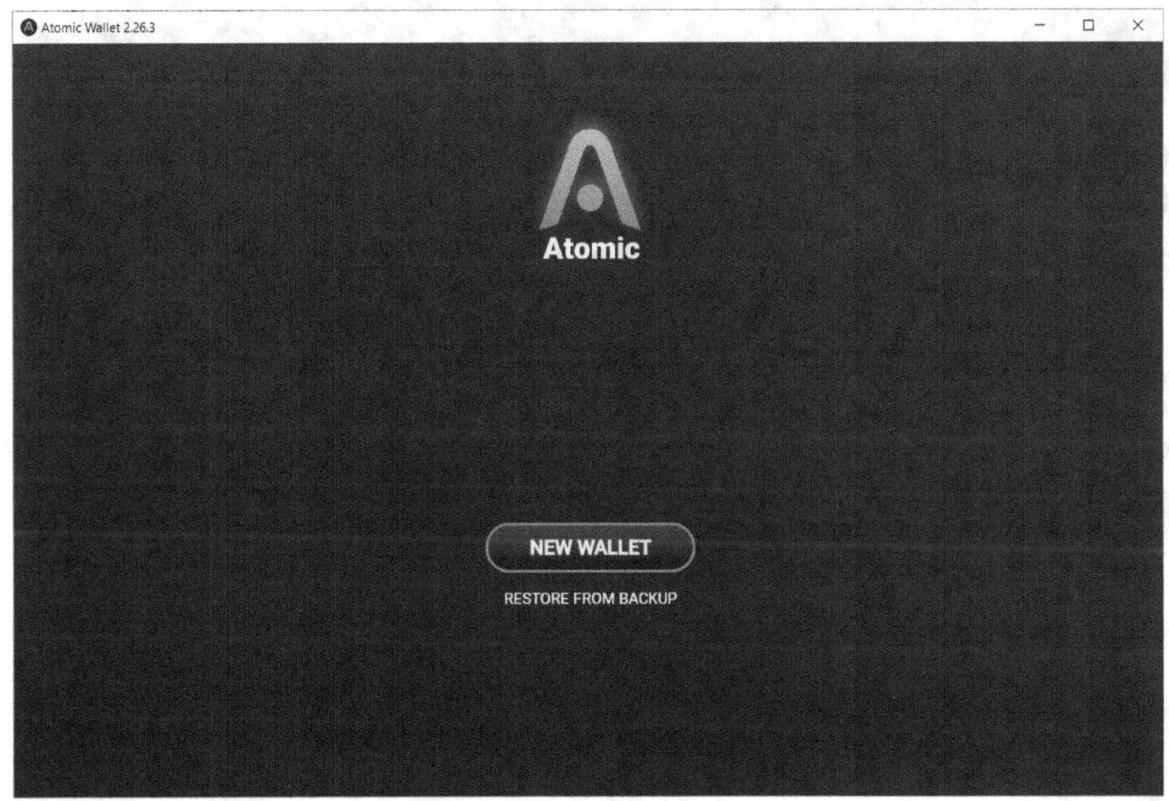

Figure 4.1 - First screen

Assuming you are using it for the first time, you probably want to create a new wallet. Pick the "New Wallet" option. The next screen asks you for a password (Figure 4.2).

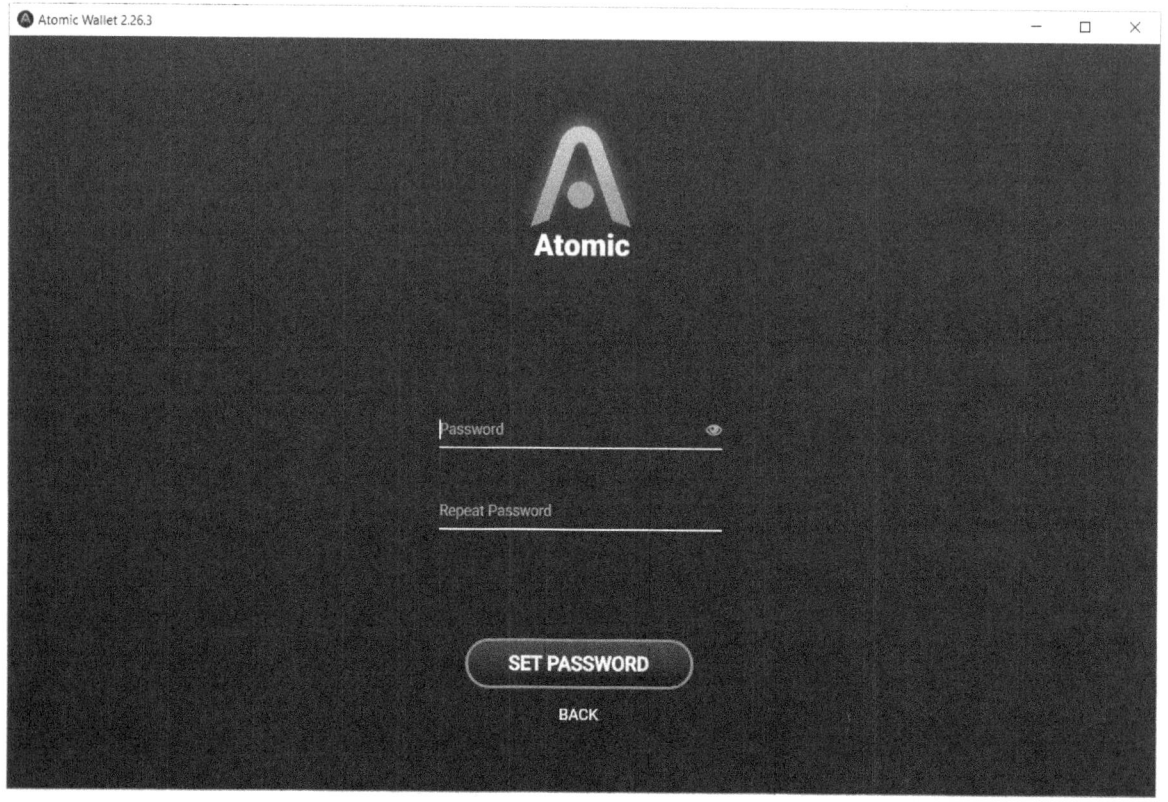

Figure 4.2 - Password creation

The purpose of this password is to grant access to the wallet itself on your Desktop. It works like the code to lock your computer or phone. It doesn't have any relation to the Public and Private keys. Whenever you close the wallet app, you will need the password to open it again.

What happens if you forget or lose this password? In this case, you will need the recovery phrase to restore the wallet.

Once you pick a password, it is time to take note of your recovery phrase. This is the most critical piece of information from a Desktop wallet perspective because this random phrase can generate your Private Keys (Figure 4.3).

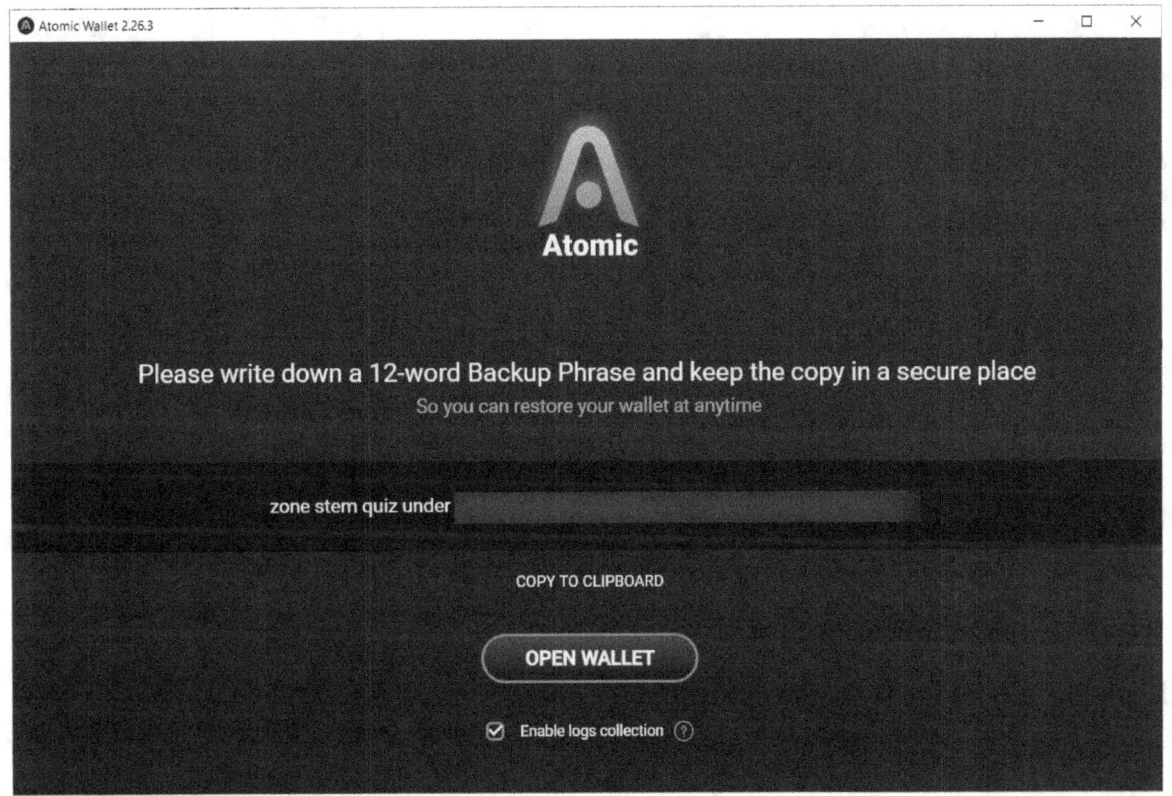

Figure 4.3 - *Backup Phrase*

Let me warn you that access to the Desktop wallet and all its funds will be lost forever if you lose this phrase. It is a serious piece of information. To prevent you from losing it, I strongly recommend writing it down on a piece of paper with at least two copies.

That is the code used to restore a wallet in case something happens to your computer. For instance, if you travel with the computer and something happens to the device, you can easily restore it. Use the phrase in the setup process to restore the wallet and all Private Keys.

Tip: *If you have multiple computers and want to use the same wallet in all of them, restore the same Phrase to have a sync wallet. You can install Atomic Wallet in all the devices and restore the Wallet with the Phrase.*

Make sure you don't write the phrase on your desktop in a plain-text file named "WalletPhrase" or anything similar. Remember, it is a way to retrieve the funds in the wallet. If someone finds it, they can restore the wallet and transfer your coins.

After you make a backup of your phrase, it is time to open the wallet. Click on the "OPEN WALLET" button for the software to process and generate all Private Keys. It generates Private Keys for all available cryptocurrencies supported by the wallet. It doesn't mean you will ever use them.

You will see a list with multiple wallets available for dozens of cryptocurrencies (Figure 4.4).

Figure 4.4 - Crypto list

If you click on the Bitcoin wallet, it opens the details for this particular wallet with options to send or receive coins (Figure 4.5).

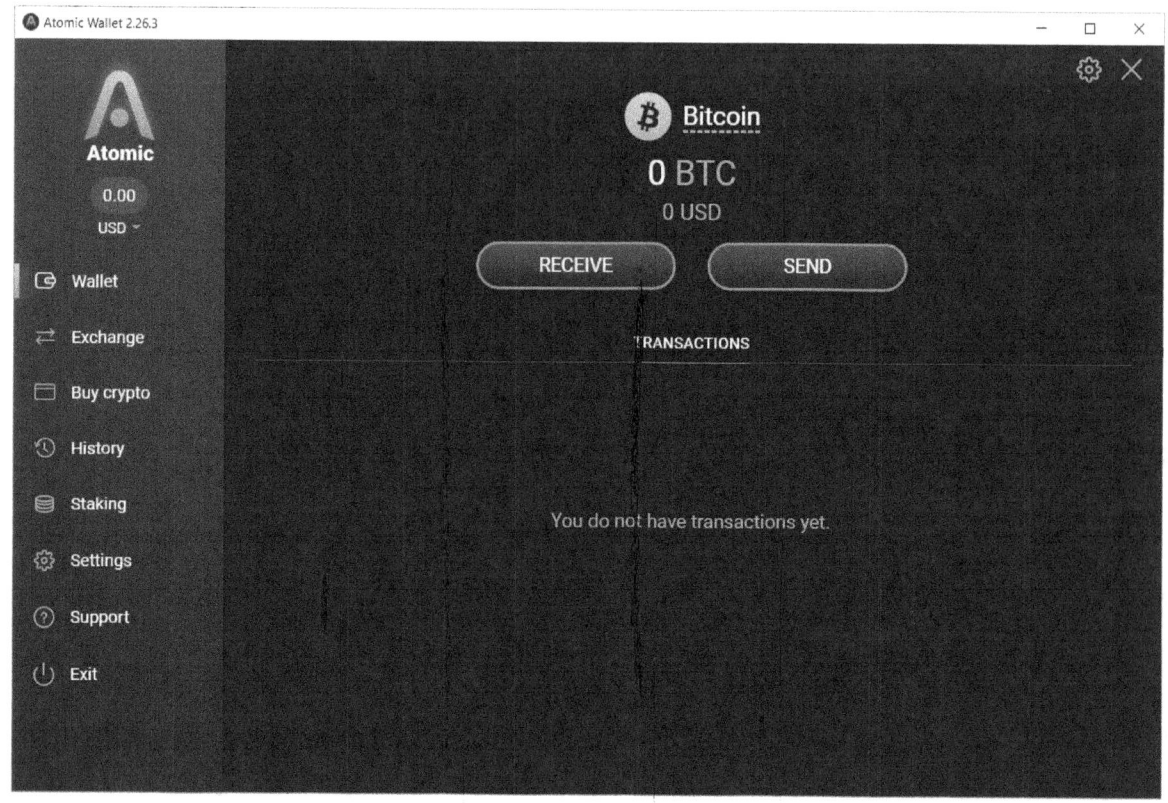

Figure 4.5 - *Bitcoin wallet*

By clicking on the Receive button, you can view and copy the Public Key (Figure 4.6).

Figure 4.6 - *Public Key*

The same applies to the Send button, where you can set a destination address and the amount you want to send (Figure 4.7).

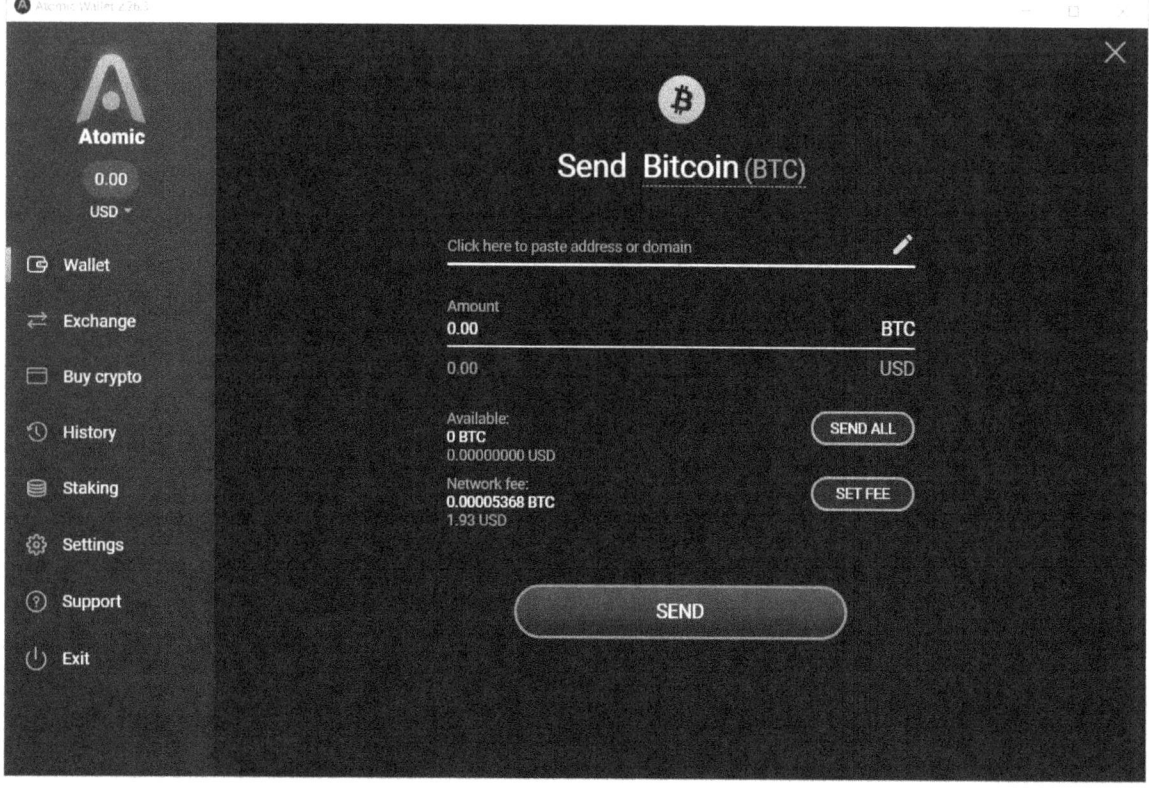

Figure 4.7 - *Send options*

Notice in Figure 4.7 that it also gives you an estimate about the fee for transfer funds. We will talk more about fees later.

Where are the Private Keys? In a software wallet like this one, you don't need to type the Private Keys. The wallet handles all the operations requiring the Private Keys for you. It reduces the chances of hacking when you don't have to type or manipulate the information.

The keys exist and are available at the settings of your wallet. Go to the settings and choose Private Keys at the top. It will require the password to display the keys (Figure 4.8).

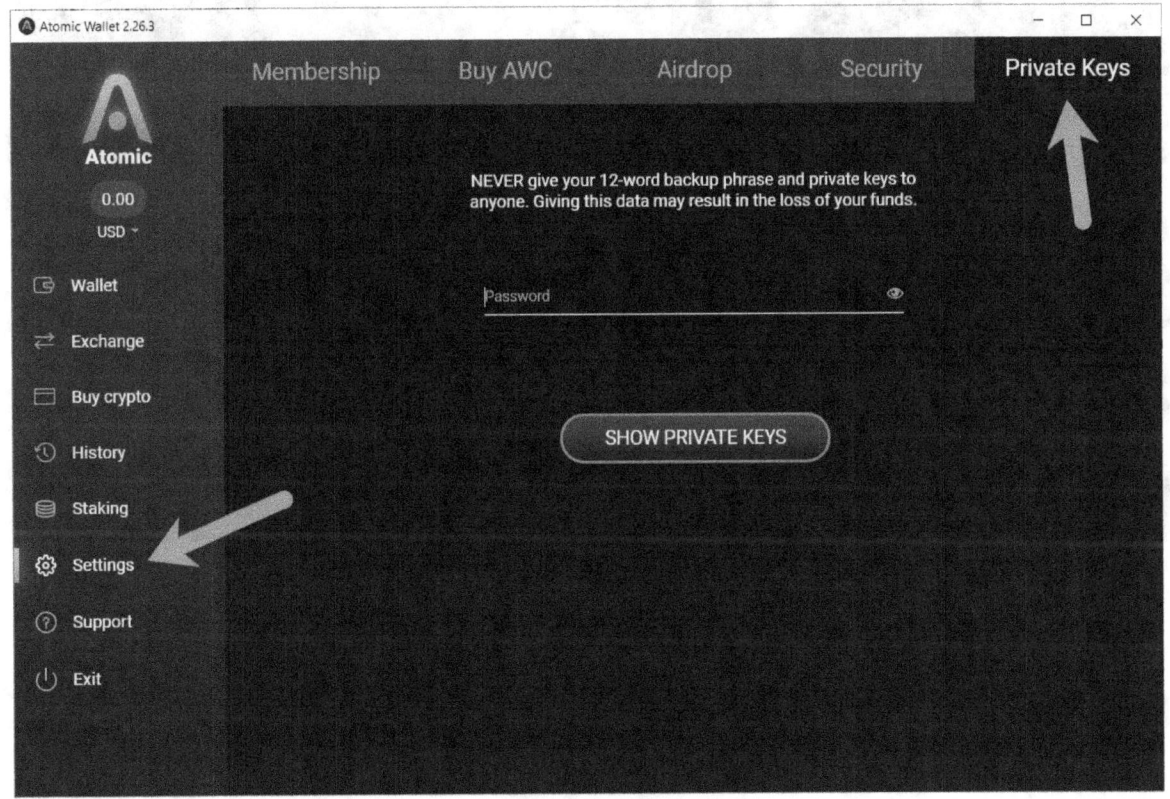

Figure 4.8 - Settings options

You can view all Private Keys for all cryptocurrencies available in the wallet (Figure 4.9).

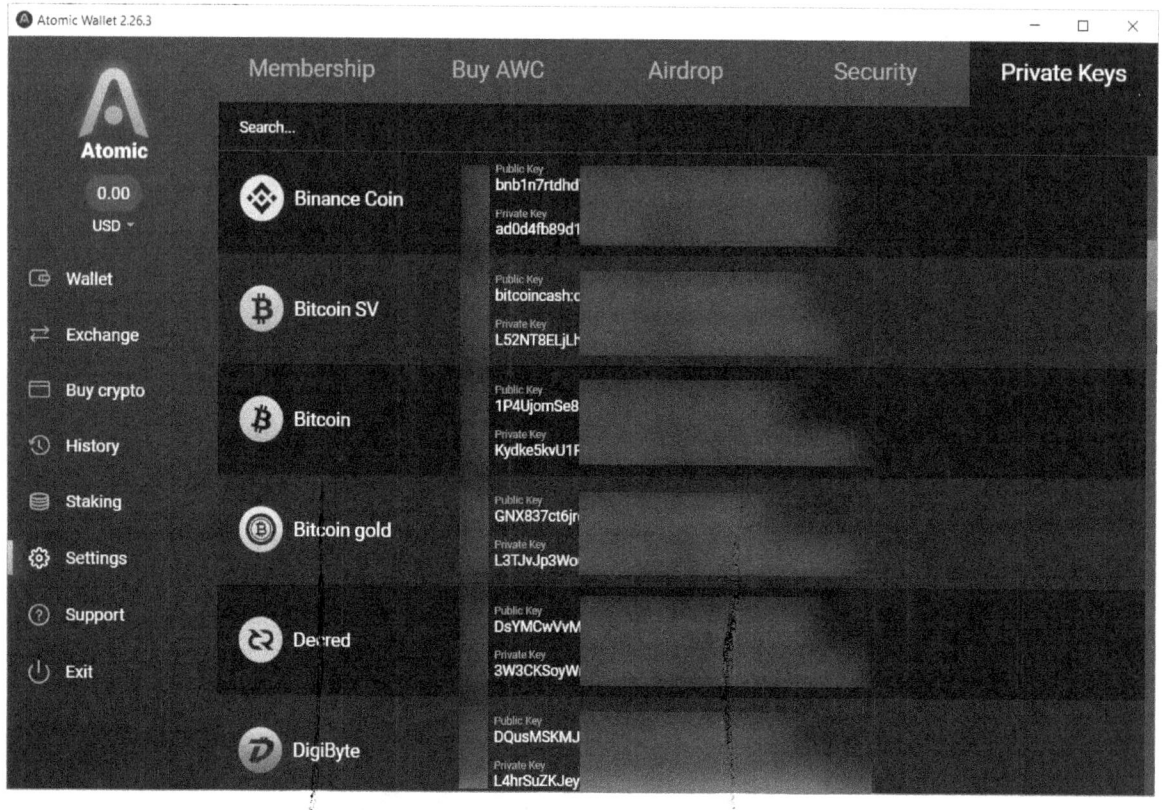

Figure 4.9 - *Private Keys list*

Among them, you find the keys to your Bitcoin wallet. Unless you need to manage or use those keys for a particular reason, there is no need to open those options.

If you just want to manage and handle Bitcoins, we can easily hide all other wallets. Use the button on the top right to filter the available currencies (Figure 4.10).

Figure 4.10 - *Filter option*

Disable everything but the Bitcoin option. Use the Apply button to activate the filter (Figure 4.11).

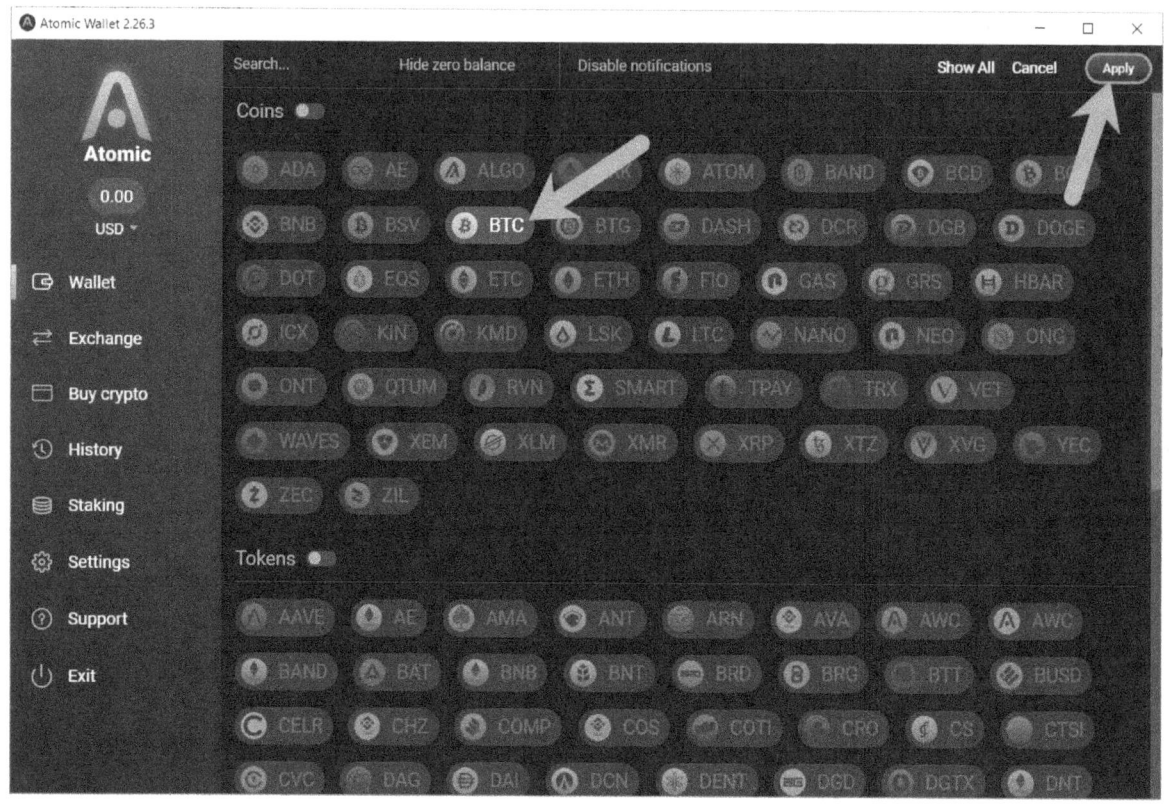

Figure 4.11 - *Apply the filter*

As a result, you can start trading and managing only Bitcoins (Figure 4.12).

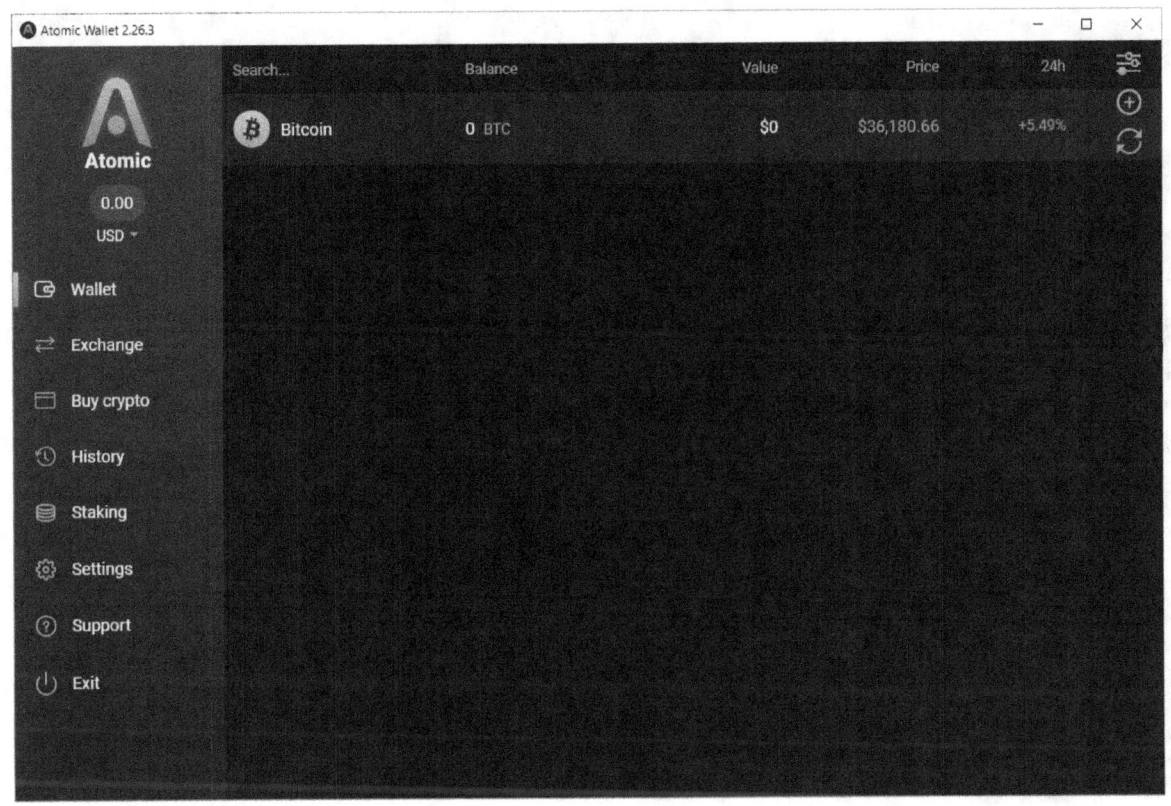

Figure 4.12 - *Bitcoin-only wallet*

Whenever you want to close the wallet, use the "Exit" button. It locks access to the wallet. You can open the same wallet later with the password (Figure 4.13).

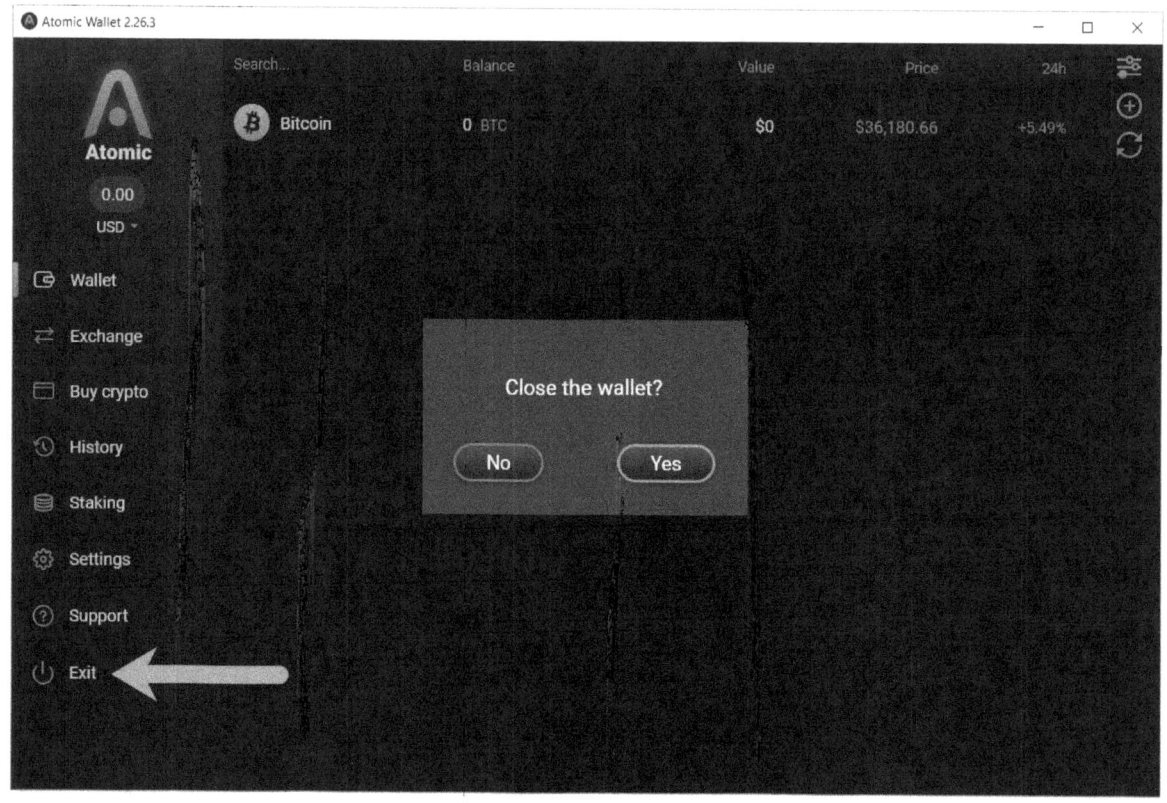

Figure 4.13 - Closing the wallet

What if you lose the password? Assuming you have a secure copy of the recovery phrase, it is easy to set a new wallet using the same phrase and restore access to the funds.

4.3.2 How to recover a wallet from a backup?

To recover access to a Desktop wallet, you only need the phrase created during the setup process. Assuming you have it saved in a secure location, the recovery process should be easy. After opening the wallet software, you will see options to:

– Open wallet

– Restore from backup

– Create wallet

If you want to retrieve an existing wallet, you must use the Restore from backup (Figure 4.14).

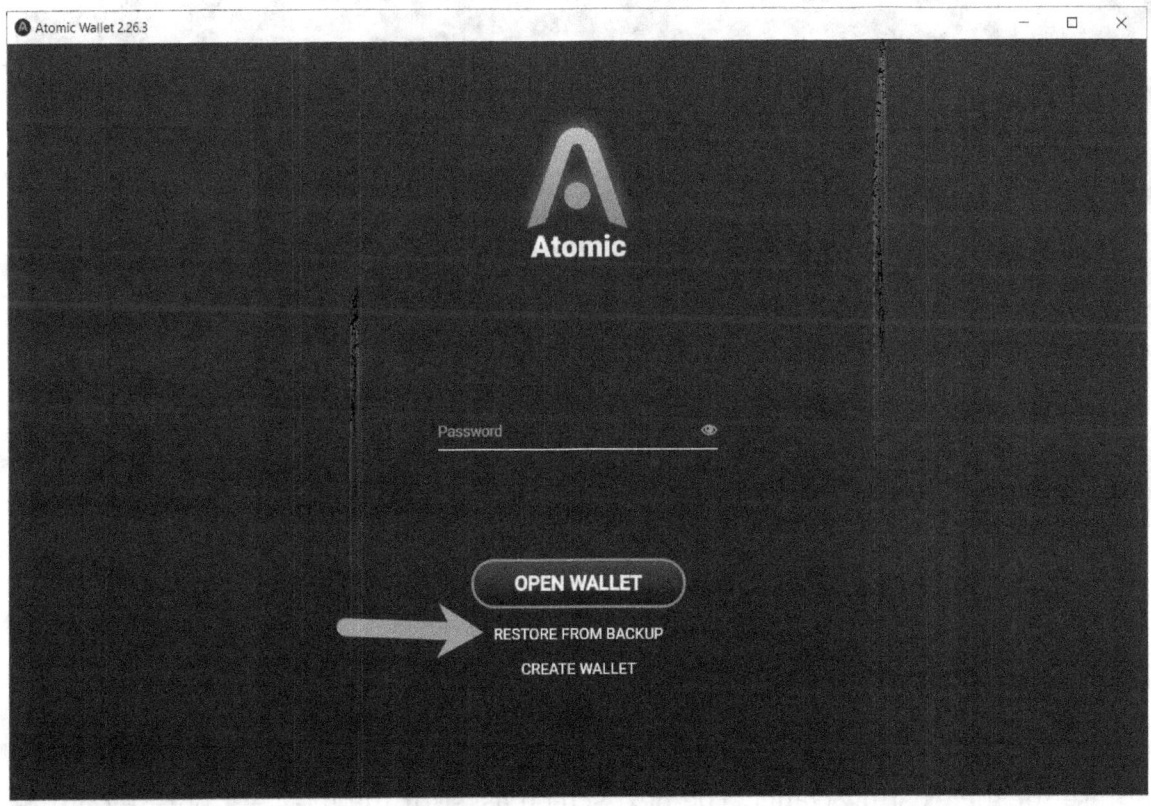

Figure 4.14 - Initial screen

For the cases where you already have an existing wallet, the software will display a warning (Figure 4.15).

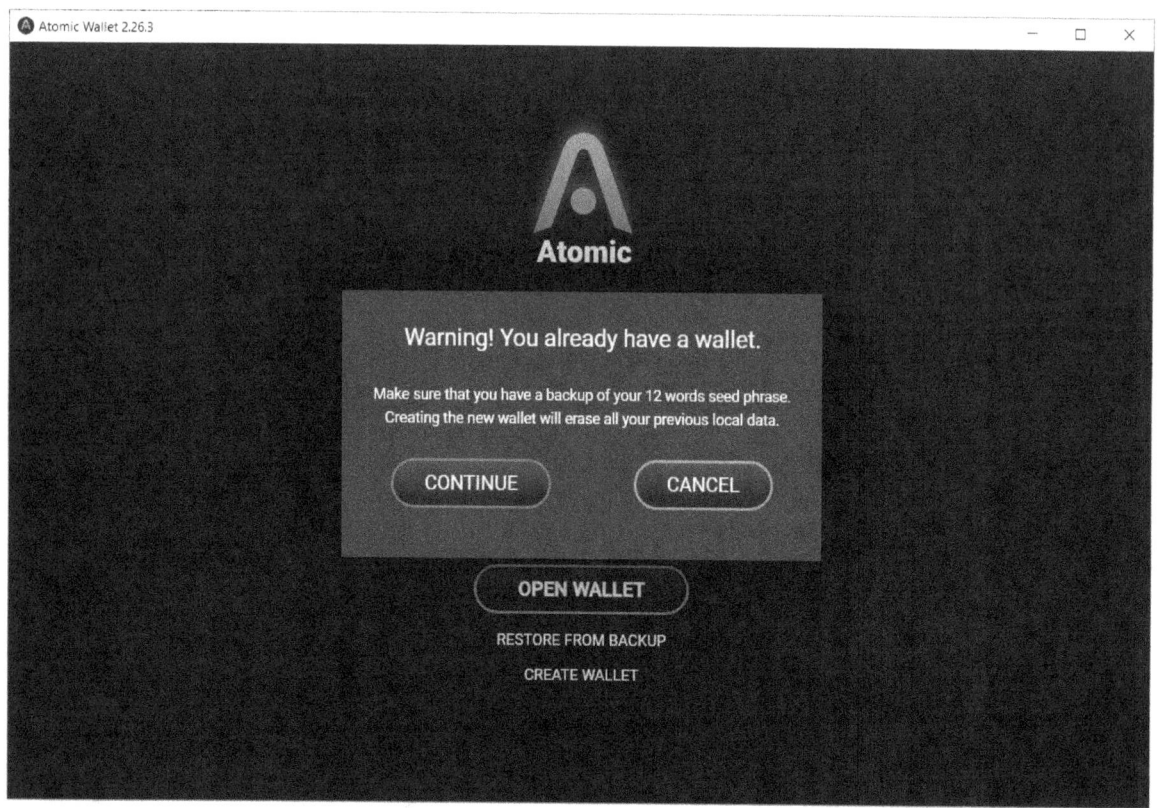

Figure 4.15 - *Warning message*

Like we mentioned before, it warns you about the need to back up the recovery phrase for the existing wallet. The next screen asks for the recovery phrase (Figure 4.16).

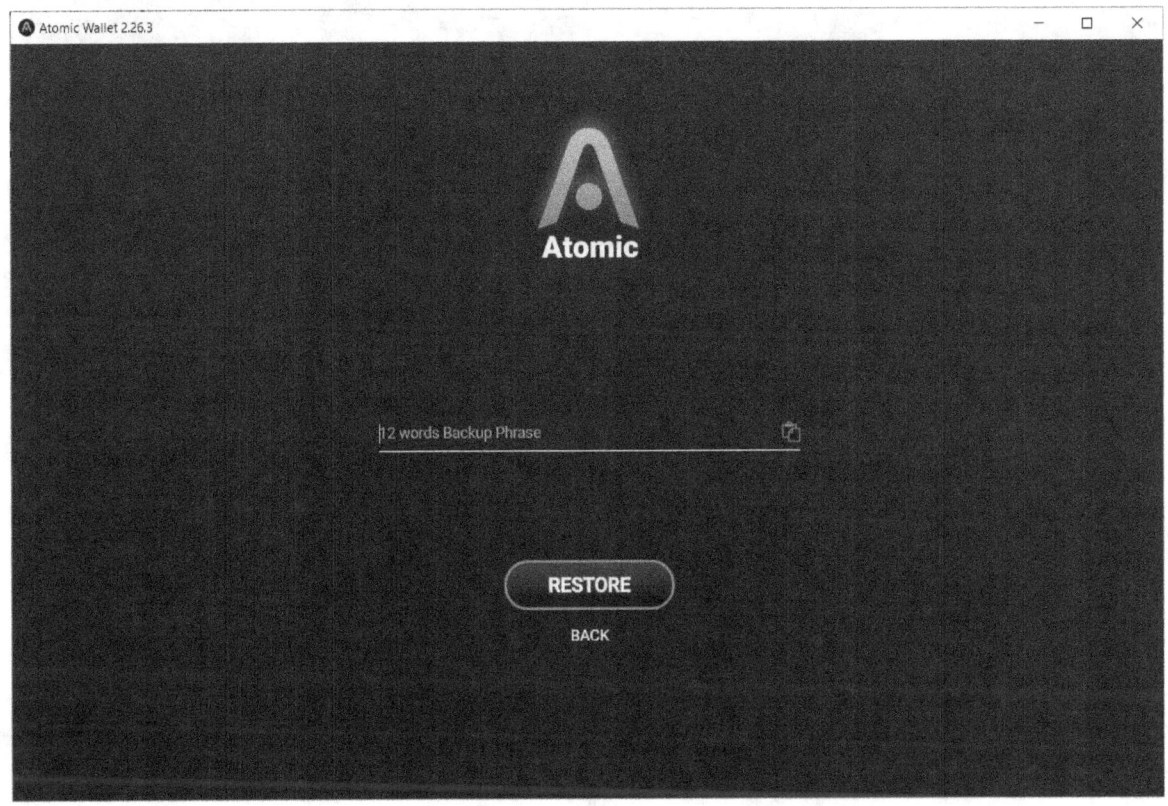

Figure 4.16 - *Restore page*

You can either type or paste the words in the same order you copied. Press the Restore button to get your wallet back. It is easy when you have the phrase saved. The wallet will be back with all funds available.

How is that possible? That is because of some of the unique features of a cryptocurrency wallet:

– The wallet doesn't hold any cryptocurrency. All coins are in the respective Blockchain.

- A wallet is a way to interact with the Blockchain ledger.

- The wallet software can rebuild the Private and Public Keys from the recovery phrase

- Once you have the Private Key back, you have access to the balance

You can use the same process to restore any wallet on different devices. In the case of Atomic Wallet, it also offers a mobile version for iOS and Android that works in the same way.

Info: We showed how a Desktop wallet works with an example and screens from Atomic wallet. Most other wallets have similar options and work similarly. They have backup and restore features using a mnemonic phrase and gives you control over multiple cryptocurrencies.

4.4 Mobile wallets

Having a Desktop wallet to trade and manage your cryptocurrency is a great alternative to use a PC or laptop as the main gateway to communicate with the Bitcoin Blockchain. But, we can't deny that we live in a mobile world, and most of our lives today happen on our smartphones. Because of that, it is most likely that you will start with a Mobile wallet.

Those are apps that work in a similar way to Desktop software but runs entirely on your phone.

If you are afraid of setting up a wallet on a phone that could be lost or stolen, you must remember:

1. The coins are not in the wallet app but the Blockchain. Losing the device doesn't mean you lose the cryptocurrency.

2. As long as you keep a secure copy of your recovery phrase, it is possible to import and rebuild the wallet on a new device.

3. Use a strong password to lock the app or a reliable biometric feature like a fingerprint scanner or FaceID. It protects the wallet from unintentional use or if you eventually share the phone with other people.

There are dozens or hundreds of apps offering Mobile wallets to store your Bitcoins and other cryptocurrencies. We have a few recommendations, but as a general rule, we always prefer open-source apps. That way, you can rely on the auditing from third-party developers to check if nothing strange is happening under the hood.

Here are some options regarding Mobile wallets:

– Trust Wallet (https://trustwallet.com)

– Exodus (https://www.exodus.io)

– Atomic Wallet (https://atomicwallet.io)

You can choose to go with a multi-platform app like Atomic Wallet and use a phrase to import Private Keys to multiple devices or choose to use a different system. Our recommendation for a mobile wallet is either Atomic Wallet or the Trust Wallet. Both of them have versions for iOS and Android.

To give you a different setup process, we can quickly show how to work with the Trust Wallet, which is open-source. The following process uses iOS, but it works the same way with Android.

After installing the App, you open it for the first time to find a setup screen. It asks you if you want to create a new pair of keys or if you already a wallet (Figure 4.17).

Figure 4.17 - Starting with the Trust Wallet

We can start creating a new wallet by choosing "Create new wallet." You will then get a warning from the app about your recovery phrase (Figure 4.18).

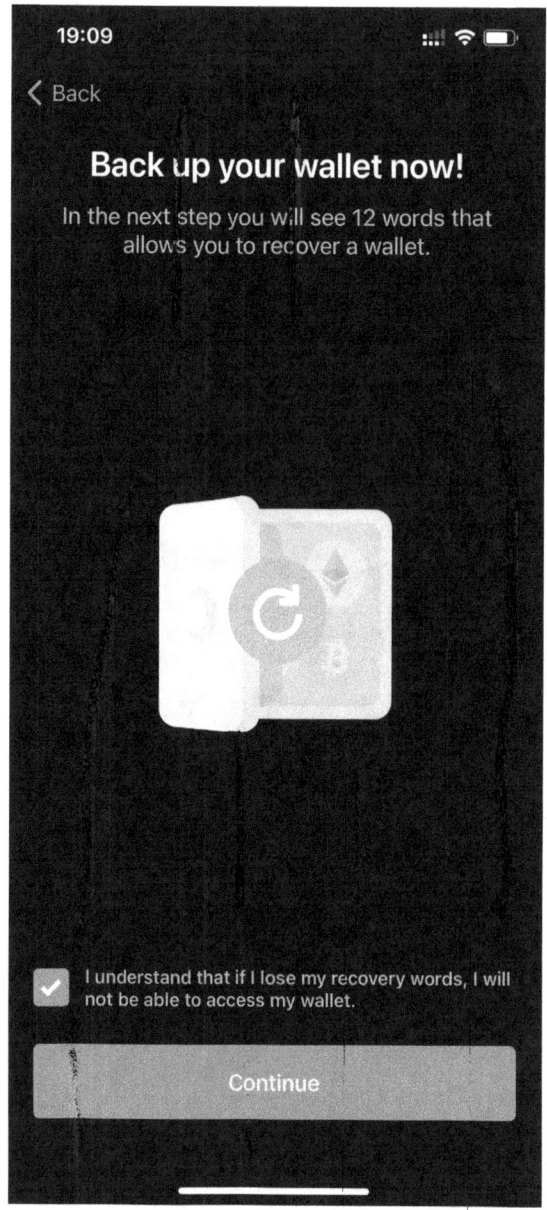

Figure 4.18 - Recovery warning

At this point, you will see the 12-word recovery phrase. Regardless of what you do, it is critical to have a secure copy of this phrase. It has the same importance as your Private Keys! I know it is becoming repetitive, but it is critical to have that backup. Otherwise, you will lose access to the wallet (Figure 4.19).

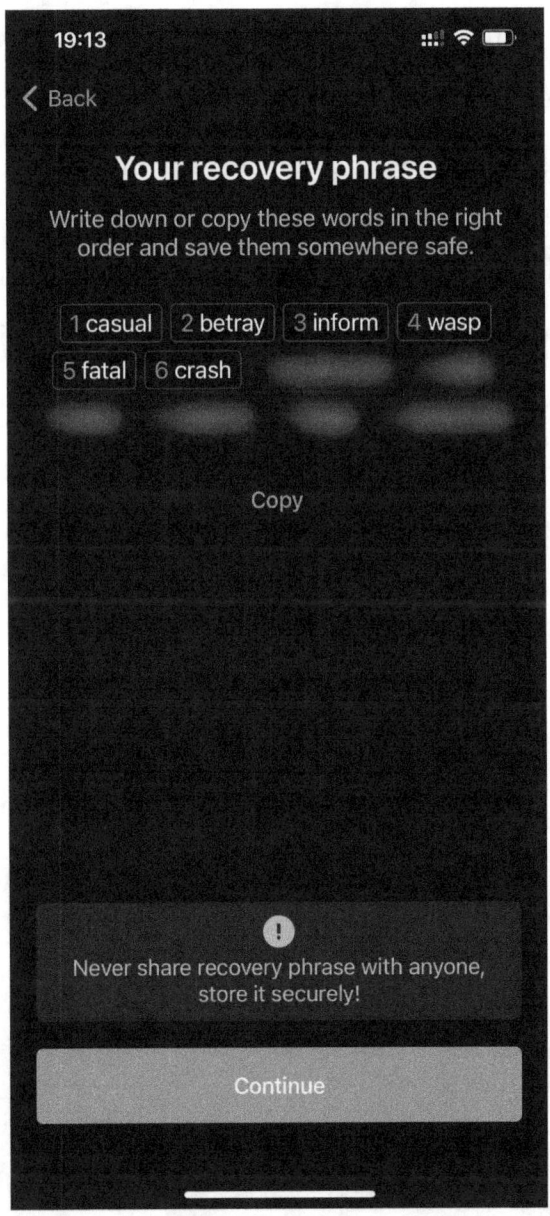

Figure 4.19 - Recovery Phrase

A convenient and dangerous way of making a copy of your phrase is taking a screenshot from this screen. Avoid doing that at all costs! Why is this dangerous?

Since your photos and images are in an unencrypted location of your phone, anyone with access to the phone can browse your images and find the 12 recovery phrase. If you upload the photos to a cloud service, the risks will be even higher!

To ensure that you have a backup copy of your phrase, the app requires you to enter the words in the same sequence on the next screen. It is another measure to make sure you have a copy of the phrase (Figure 4.20).

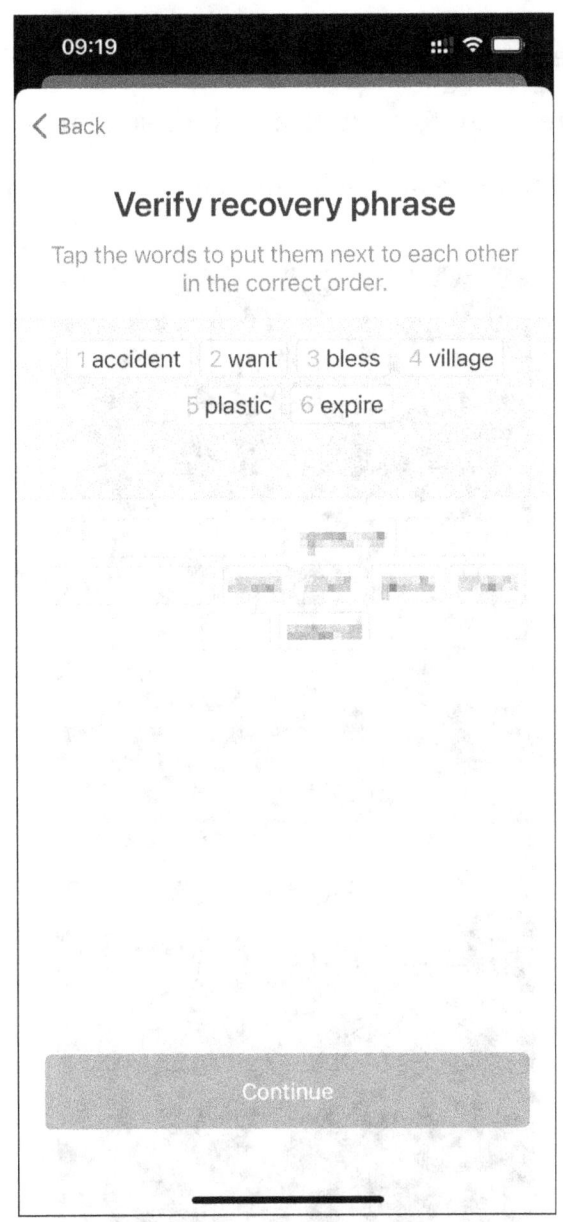

Figure 4.20 - Entering the Phrase

If you successfully enter the phrase in the verification process, the wallet creates your keys, and you are ready to start receiving or sending coins. Like many other crypto wallets, you can manage and hold dozens of existing coins (Figure 4.21).

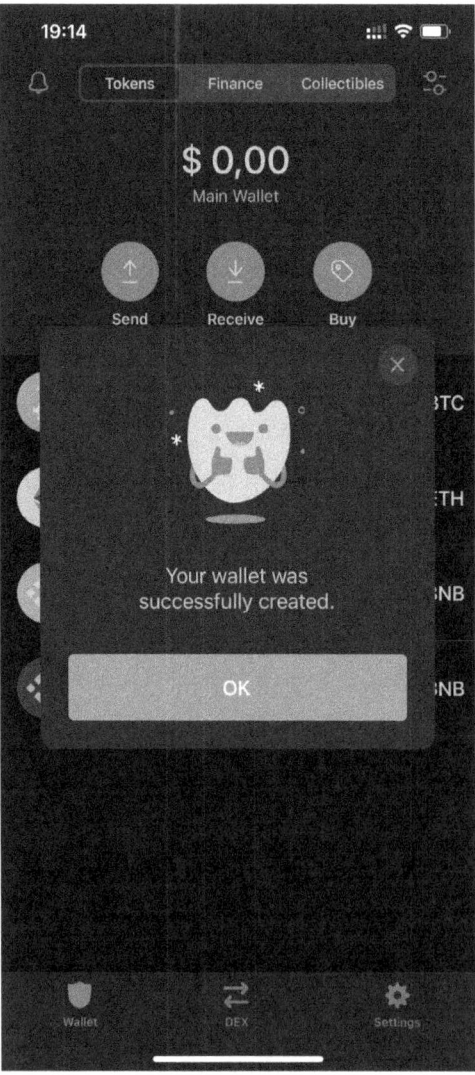

Figure 4.21 - *Confirmation screen*

You will see a list with all available cryptocurrencies supported (Figure 4.21).

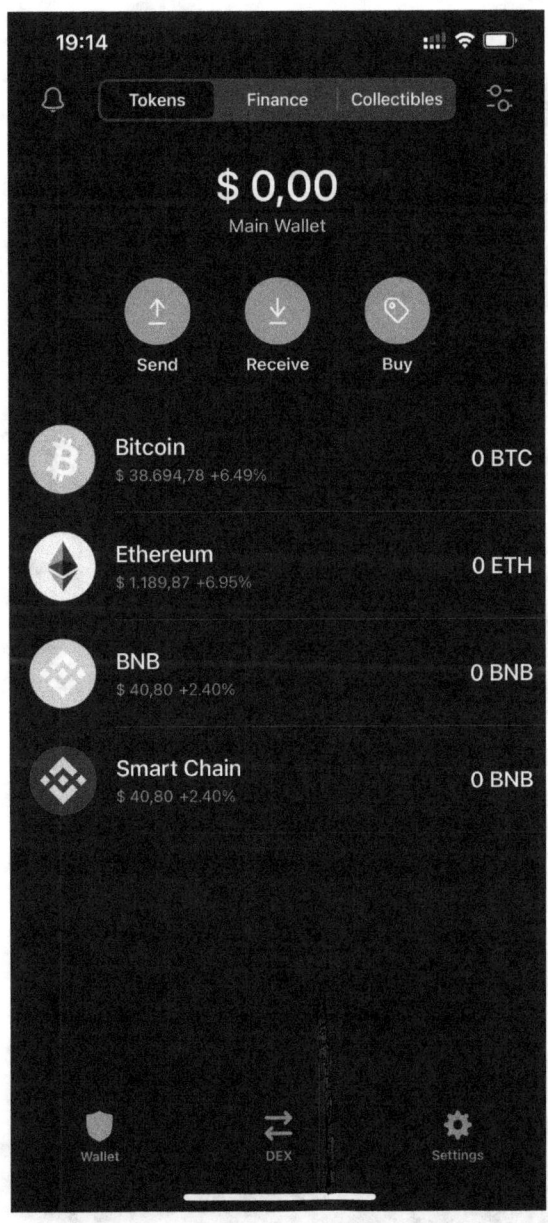

Figure 4.22 - *Available wallets*

By tapping at the Bitcoin wallet, you can see options to send and receive coins (Figure 4.23).

Figure 4.23 - *Send and receive coins*

Inside the wallet app's settings, you find additional tools and options to add more wallets with unique phrases and Keys. You can see the current wallet at the top, and by tapping at the wallet name, you can add more of them (Figure 4.24).

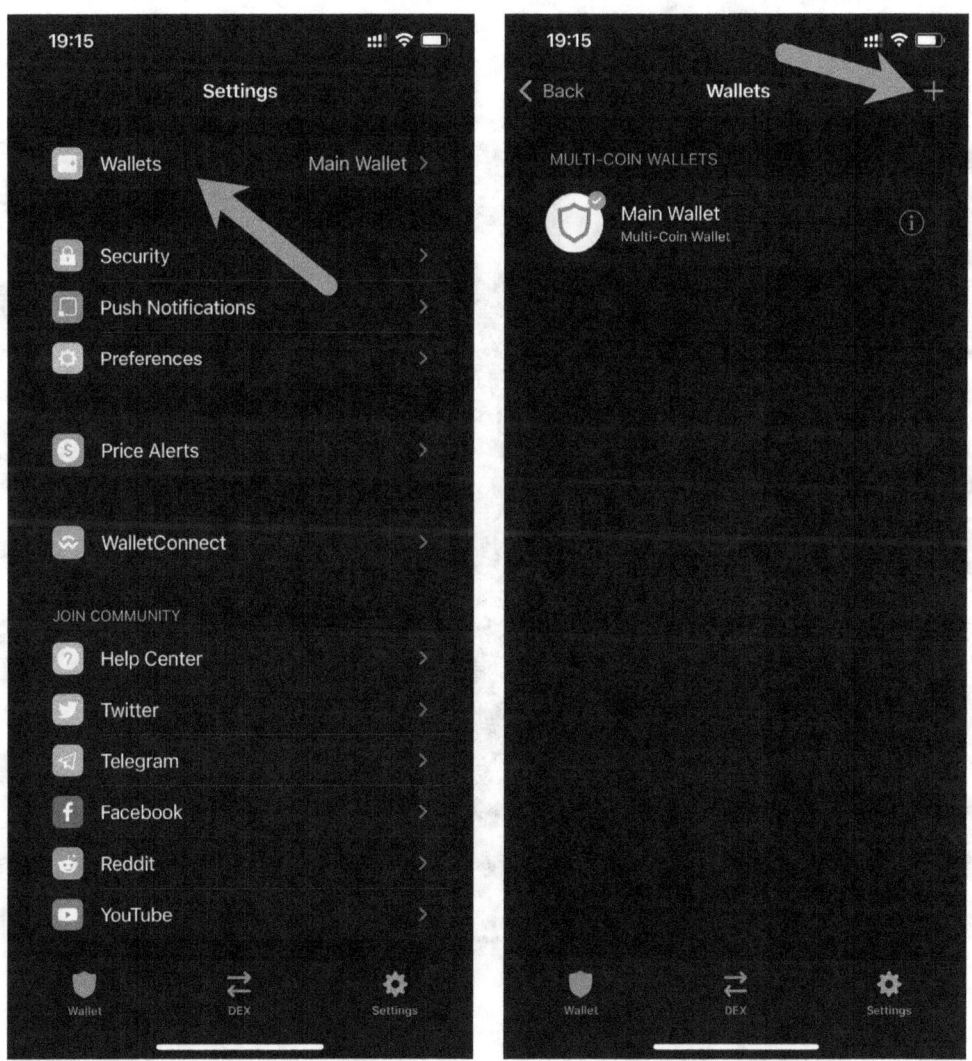

Figure 4.24 - Adding new wallets

In the security settings for the wallet, you can make the app much more secure. Like the password added to the Desktop wallet, we can create a PIN code to restrict the wallet. That is helpful when you have other people handling the phone. For instance, if your kids use the phone to watch videos or play games, it is wise to add this layer of protection (Figure 4.25).

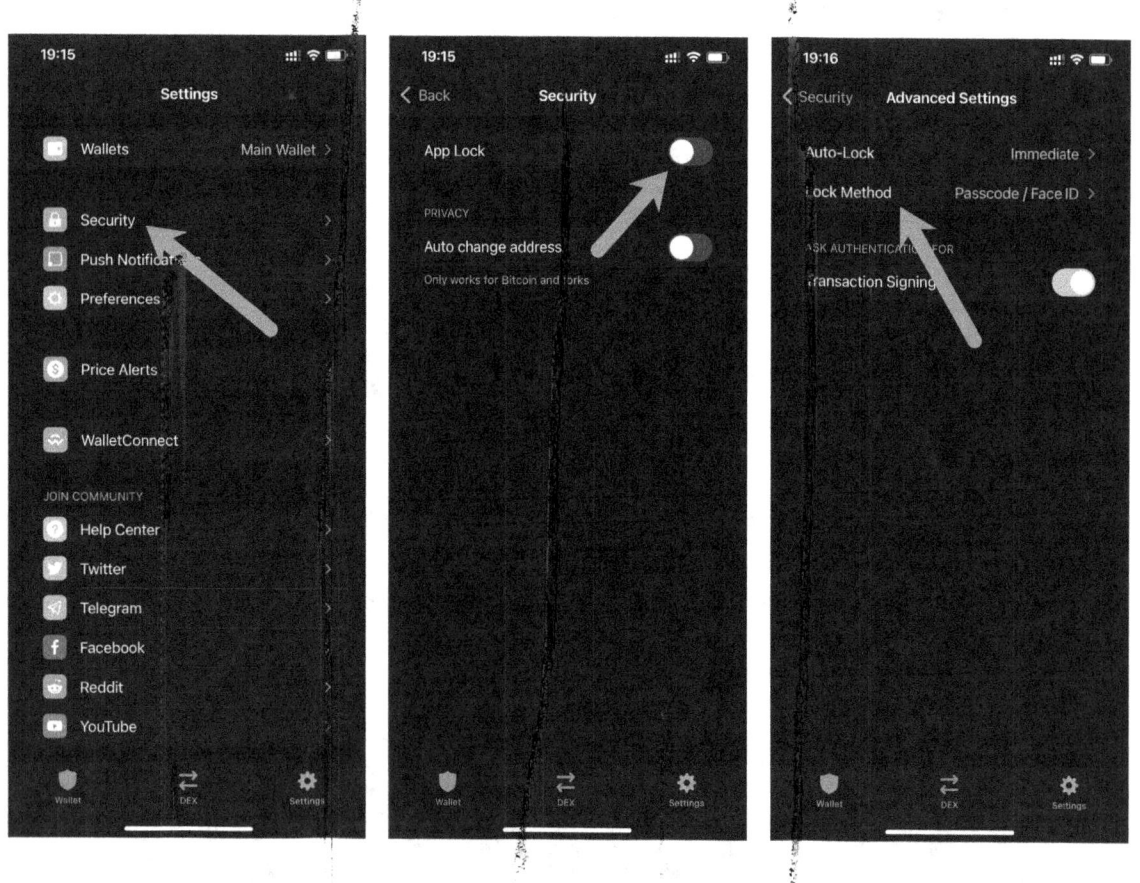

Figure 4.25 - Advanced settings

It is also possible to enable FaceID or Fingerprint lock to add even more security to the process. Finally, by enabling the "Transaction signing" option, it will demand either the PIN or biometric authentication to sign transactions and move coins out of your wallet.

The use of those features depends on your phone having them available.

4.4.1 Mobile wallet security

The mobile wallet offers a convenient way of managing your cryptocurrencies with something that most people today have in their pockets, which is a smartphone. However, it also represents a potential risk. Due to those wallets' mobile nature, there is always a chance for you to lose access to the device.

You can lose it somewhere or have it stolen. In case that happens, you should always:

– Have a secure copy of the recovery phrase (Not on your phone)

– Make sure you have the phone locked with a strong passcode or biometric feature

– Use a PIN or biometric authentication to open the wallet app

– Do not keep unencrypted copies of your phrase on the phone, like a screenshot

If you fail to follow any one of those steps, you will be at risk of having someone else finding the phrase and steal your funds. Having an unprotected mobile wallet would be like writing the PIN of your credit card on paper and place it inside your wallet next to the card.

Info: The same rules apply to Desktop wallets in laptops, which you can also lose.

4.4.2 Double-check the wallet app

You can choose multiple wallet options for your phone by going to either the App-Store or PlayStore and searching for "Crypto Wallet." It returns dozens of options. Make sure you pick one with good reviews and ratings because some apps are trying to use names that look like legitimate projects to steal your coins.

Always double-check the app name before entering any sensitive information!

4.5 Web-based wallets

For the cases where you want to use a web-based solution to interact with the Blockchain, we have the wallets designed to work online only. Those are popular wallets that offer both a convenient and fast way to store and trade Bitcoins and other cryptocurrencies. The vast majority of those wallets are part of an exchange.

We will discuss more about exchanges in the next chapter, but we can start by saying that those wallets offer a high risk for anyone leaving a balance there in the long term. Unlike wallets using local storage to handle your Private Keys or recovery phrase, you don't have access to either of them with a web-based wallet.

Instead of managing your Private Keys, you give away control over the funds to the server running the wallet. It is a custodian based solution. Is this a big deal? Should you care about not having control over the Private Keys?

There is a popular saying among cryptocurrency users:

`Not your keys, not your coins`

It means that if you are not the person in control of the Private Keys, someone else could easily spend or transfer all your balance. Imagine that you will open a bank account, and instead of having the PIN and passwords to control your money, you hire an intermediate company to do that for you. You have to ask them to do anything related to your money.

That is how a web-based wallet works. You usually register a user account with a traditional username and password, and that is it—no access to a Private Key.

If the wallet system has a security flaw, hackers could easily find the Private Keys and transfer all the funds.

Did it happen before? Yes, many times! The problem here is that you must trust the security of your wallet provider. Usually, those systems have huge security problems or are vulnerable to attacks from hackers. Of course, some web-based wallets have no public history of hacks. But, it is never 100% secure.

Info: *Even with all those risks, a recent study estimates that 60% of all cryptocurrencies are in web-based wallets.*

What people usually do is to move a balance to the web-based wallet for trading purposes, and as soon you finish trading, you can take it out to a location where you control the Private Keys.

Some of the most popular options regarding web-based wallets are:

– Coinbase (https://www.coinbase.com)

– Kraken (https://www.kraken.com)

– Binance (https://www.binance.com)

Those are just a few of the options available online with web-based wallets. You can send and withdraw coins from each of them to a Desktop, mobile, hardware, or paper wallet. There are hundreds of options available online to help you manage cryptocurrencies.

When using a web-based wallet, you should consider a few things:

– Security

– Easiness of sending and withdrawing

– Privacy concerns

If you want to keep a wallet and balance in Bitcoins in one of those services, it may be good to know that they make Bitcoin less private. Most of those companies providing web-based wallets must comply with the recent laws and regulations about crypto trading. A lot of them require proof of identification to give you access to their services.

It will be possible to trace back your cryptocurrency activities after providing identification. If you want full privacy, you must avoid those types of wallets.

The purpose of those wallets is mainly for trading cryptocurrencies. Do not use them as a savings account. Unlike a non-custodial wallet that helps you keep all sensitive information in your possession, a web-based solution is a Hot wallet that maintains Private Keys in a central server.

It is a great target for hackers! If they breach their security, it will be possible to gain access to thousands of coins.

Info: There are multiple cases of exchanges that went out of business after suffering an attack from hackers and losing all coins stored there. Do extensive research before picking one of those wallets.

4.6 Hardware wallets

If you want to go serious about cryptocurrencies and long term deposits, you should start thinking about using a hardware wallet. That is one of the safest and reliable cold storage options. A hardware wallet keeps your Private Keys in a secure and encrypted device that looks like a flash drive or small card (Figure 4.26).

Figure 4.26 - Hardware wallet examples

Why is that a secure way of handling and managing cryptocurrencies? We can list a few aspects of a hardware wallet that gives you peace of mind when working with cryptocurrencies:

– **It is a Cold Wallet:** The device is always offline by design, which means you have a low risk of getting hacked.

– **Private keys are never exposed:** The keys inside the device are never in real danger because they never get exposed to the internet.

– **To steal your coins, a thief needs the device:** To gain access to the wallet, a hacker or thief must get your device in the first place.

You can replace the wallet if you lost or break it: You can regain access to the wallet if the device stops working or you lose it. By using the recovery phrase, it is possible to restore a lost or broken device.

It is a type of device that gives you peace of mind when storing and managing a wallet with a high balance!

Unlike many software-based wallets that we listed in this chapter, you must buy the device to start using a hardware wallet. Some of the cheapest options start with US$ 50-60. There are other options with fancy features like color screens and even Bluetooth connectivity, which could increase the price to something close to US$ 200.

Two popular brands among cryptocurrency holders are from companies like:

– Legder

– Trezor

Each brand offers unique features and compatibility with hundreds of cryptocurrencies besides Bitcoins. Before using any hardware wallet, do your research and read reviews to find the best option.

4.6.1 When should you use a hardware wallet?

If you are planning to use Bitcoins for savings, a hardware wallet is a great option. Because you can place the device in a secure location in your house, office, or even a bank safe, when the time comes to move the coins out of the wallet, you can plug the hardware wallet in your computer to start a transaction.

Should you invest in a hardware wallet? For small balances up to 1000 USD in cryptocurrencies, it might not worth getting a hardware wallet. You would need to spend almost 5% to 20% of your balance on a device.

However, after that amount and starting with balances of US$ 5000 or more, you should definitively think about getting a hardware wallet. It is by far the most secure and reliable way of protecting your investment.

Tip: If I had to recommend a wallet to a beginner, it would probably be a combination of a hardware wallet for long-term investments and a mobile version. That way, you can unite a Hot Wallet's convenience in your smartphone with a Cold Wallet solution like a physical device for maximum security.

4.6.2 The risks of a hardware wallet

Are there any security risks in a hardware wallet? Yes, it is not risk-free. If you do a quick search on Youtube, you might even find disturbing videos with people showing how to hack such devices. To make it work, they need physical access to the wallet and assume the manufacturer won't make updates to make them more secure.

The real risk of a hardware wallet is with the mishandling of your recovery phrase. If you give away that phrase, a scammer can access your cryptocurrencies even with no physical access to the device.

How is that possible? Remember that with the recovery phrase, a wallet software generates all Public and Private Keys. The purpose of this phrase is to work as a backup for the wallet in case you lose or break the device.

Info: Usually, those hardware wallets require longer recovery phrases with 24 words instead of the usual 12 from a software wallet.

A typical way of getting people to disclose the recovery phrase is with a phone call. After discovering that you have a hardware wallet for cryptocurrencies, a scammer can call you and say he is from the wallet manufacturer's tech support. He will claim that there is a problem with the device and request the recovery phrase for verification.

If you give him the phrase, it will be possible to clone your hardware wallet and transfer all the funds.

A hardware wallet requires the same type of care regarding your recovery phrase!

4.7 Paper wallet

The last type of wallet is a paper wallet. As we described in the last chapter with the useful bitaddress.org website, you can create a pair of Private and Public keys to generate the ultimate cold storage wallet.

If you print the results of your wallet following the steps described in the previous chapter, like disconnecting the computer from the internet and print the keys as the only copy, you will have an incredibly secure wallet.

Should you use it? The short answer; no. For beginners and even advanced users of cryptocurrencies, a paper wallet offers more risks than benefits. Having the wallet on a piece of paper that you can lose in many different ways is a security nightmare.

If you decide to hide it in your home, you will be at risk of having the wallet lost in multiple ways:

– A fire

– Flood

– Your kids might find the paper to draw

– Your dog can destroy the paper

– Someone can put it in the trash

Unlike software or hardware wallets that offers ways for backing up the Private Key, you will lose access to the wallet forever if something happens to the paper. There is no recovery phrase for the paper wallet.

A lot can happen with a paper wallet. Unless you know all the risks and are ready to accept them, stay away from this solution and go with a hardware wallet for long term storage.

Info: *Another downside of a paper wallet is that it doesn't offer software convenience to interact with the Blockchain. Once you need to move the funds, you will have to import the Private Keys somewhere to either sell the coins or transfer them to another wallet.*

What is next?

If you still didn't create a wallet after reading this chapter, now it is time to start making wallets and tests their respective features. From all of those options, I believe the easiest type is a mobile wallet. With your phone, it is possible to download and install an app that creates multiple cryptocurrency wallets.

As a way to practice your security and backup management, take a piece of paper and write the recovery phrase outside your device. Make sure you have it in a secure and reliable location. You should also add a PIN or password to lock access to the wallet app.

Remember that losing the recovery phrase can put your balance at risk. There is no one to call for help if that happens. The purpose of the system is to make it harder for people to break into the wallet. It means the wallet provider can't access or reset the recovery phrase in case you lose it.

Chapter 5 - Managing Bitcoins and network fees

One of Bitcoin's highlights is that it runs on a decentralized network, which is the opposite of many financial institutions with centralized structures. Even with such different working models, both systems share a common aspect. They cost money to maintain. Who pays the bill?

In this case, anyone trying to make payments or transactions in the Bitcoin network must pay a small fee. The following chapter explains how you can manage and move coins between wallets and estimate the costs.

Knowing the fee model is essential to have a better understanding of confirmation speeds in the network.

Here is a list of what you will learn:

– How to manage Bitcoins in a wallet

– Sending and receiving Bitcoins

– Bitcoin fees: How to calculate and estimate fees

– The benefits of SegWit transactions

– Manipulating fees to change conformation speeds

5.1 Managing Bitcoins in a wallet

A wallet that holds cryptocurrency Private Keys, like the ones presented in the previous chapter, are great to help you manage your coins. If you installed one of those wallets on your computer or phone, it is time to take a look at how you can move the funds in and out to see the "flow" of Bitcoins.

Before we start explaining how to transfer and manage funds to a wallet, it is important to remind you about some facts about a Bitcoin wallet:

  – The wallet is a way to interact with the Blockchain and the Bitcoin ledger

  – Your wallet doesn't hold any coins

  – All coins (Tokens) remain in the Blockchain

  – The only thing belonging to you is the Private Key or recovery phrase

  – Transactions processed in the Bitcoin ledger are irreversible

If you want to follow all the steps described in the chapter, you should ensure that you have a safe copy of either the Private Keys or recovery phrase. That is your only backup for the wallet data.

5.2 Sending Bitcoins

One of the first types of transactions that you probably will want to perform with Bitcoins is withdrawing a balance from a web-based wallet. That happens when you buy Bitcoins from a place like an exchange. Keeping your coins in the exchange wallet is a bad idea, and we will discuss that even further in chapters 6 and 7, you probably will want to withdraw them.

Imagine that you want to start your savings in Bitcoins, and the first thing you do is go to an exchange and buy some coins. After making an account at the exchange and buying the coins with fiat currency like Dollars or Euros, the coins appear in your wallet.

Having the balance in the exchange wallet is convenient, and for some people, it might even bring peace of mind because you think that they are safe there with a high technological and secure way of protecting the wallets. The majority of exchanges work in a custodian-based, and you will have the coins attached to your user account. You don't have access to the Private Keys.

A lot of exchanges keep a couple of Private Keys controlling the vast majority of their Bitcoins. If one of those keys leaks, it means thousands of Bitcoins are at risk.

Like we mentioned before, a common saying among cryptocurrency investors is:

```
Not your keys, not your coins
```

To move your Bitcoins out of the exchange, you need another wallet with a Public Key. A convenient type of wallet for this operation is a mobile app. Once you have the mobile app installed with all the backups and a copy of either the Private Key or recovery phrase, we can begin.

In the mobile wallet, you can open the Receiving section to view your Public Key (Figure 5.1).

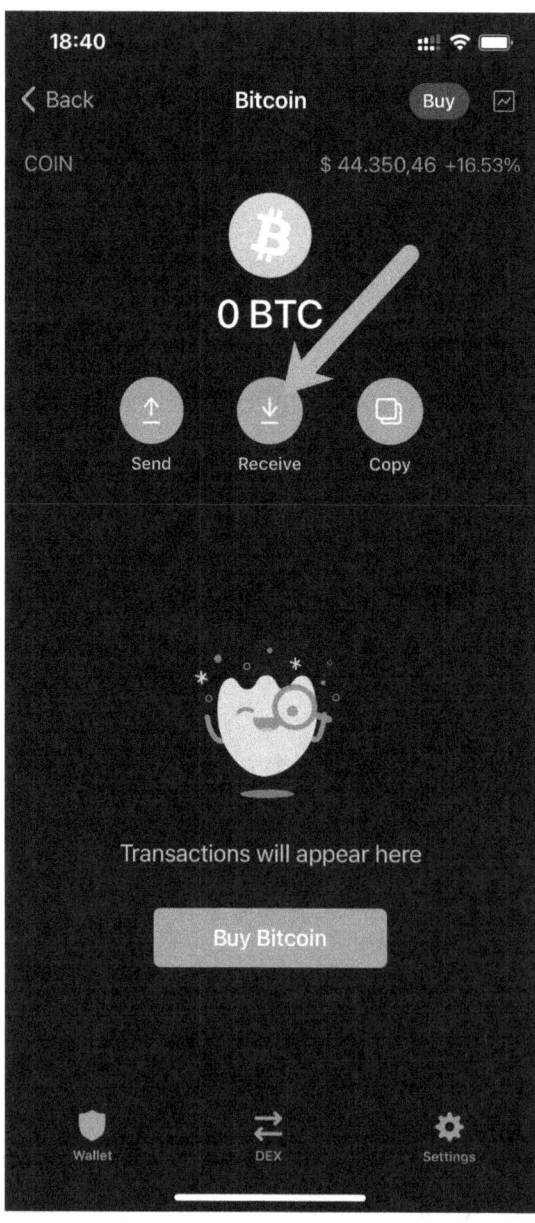

Figure 5.1 - Receiving option

That is the address you use to receive coins from other wallets and is perfectly safe to share it with anyone. No one can control the coins associated with the wallet by knowing only the Public Key (Figure 5.2).

Figure 5.2 - *Public Key address*

As you can see from this wallet app and many other locations, you will find a QR Code for most of the keys. The app makes it easy to use your phone camera to scan any address. Whenever you have to make a transfer, use the QR Code to make your life easier.

In the exchange withdrawal settings, you can type or paste the Public Address of your mobile wallet (Figure 5.3).

Cryptocurrency Withdrawals

Select cryptocurrency

BTC Bitcoin

Destination BTC address

Address label (optional)

Amount in BTC

Fee 0.0005 BTC
Total 0.0005 BTC

Available 0.00000000

Authenticate and withdraw

We batch withdrawals and send them out every 15 minutes.
Withdrawals of large amounts may take up to 48 hours to process.

Figure 5.3 - Type the destination wallet

Think about the Public Address of your Bitcoin wallet as if it were the account and routing numbers of your bank. After double-checking to see if the numbers are all correct, you can hit the send button.

You may also notice that the exchange will charge you a fee to process the transfer despite the number of coins entered for your withdrawal. It is something that you can't avoid or control when using an exchange. Keep that in mind when you choose one to buy or trade cryptocurrencies. In the long term, it may add up a lot to your savings.

Tip: *In some cases, since the withdrawal fee has a fixed cost, it may be a good strategy to withdraw only large amounts of Bitcoin to save in fees.*

Depending on your exchange's security settings, you may have to perform additional steps to withdraw coins from a wallet. For instance, in my case, I was using an exchange that required a second verification by e-mail.

In the e-mail they send all information regarding the withdraw like:

– Amount of coins

– Destination wallet

– Details of the sender operation

This is a welcome security measure to ensure only you can withdraw funds from a wallet if someone hacks your exchange account. They would need access to your e-mail to withdraw funds.

5.2.1 Processing a transfer

When getting funds out of a web-based wallet from an exchange, you may have to wait a few minutes to start processing that particular transaction. Each exchange has rules about that type of procedure, but most of them start small transactions related to coins in a couple of minutes. They wait until a lot of people try to withdraw funds and run them in a batch.

On the exchange transaction page, you will see the status for this transfer as "Waiting to be processed" (Figure 5.4).

Withdrawal Overview				Withdrawals older than 90 days
		Type ⌄		Status ⌄
ID	Date	Type	Amount	Status
9490254	Jan. 15, 2021 7:04 p.m. UTC	Bitcoin (BTC)	0.00081575 BTC	Waiting to be processed ✕

Figure 5.4 - *Transaction status*

What if you go to the mobile wallet? At this point, if you try to refresh the mobile wallet app, nothing appears there in the transaction history.

A few minutes later, after refreshing the wallet app, you will see the transfer there. In my case, it took only 6 minutes for the transaction to appear in my wallet (Figure 5.5).

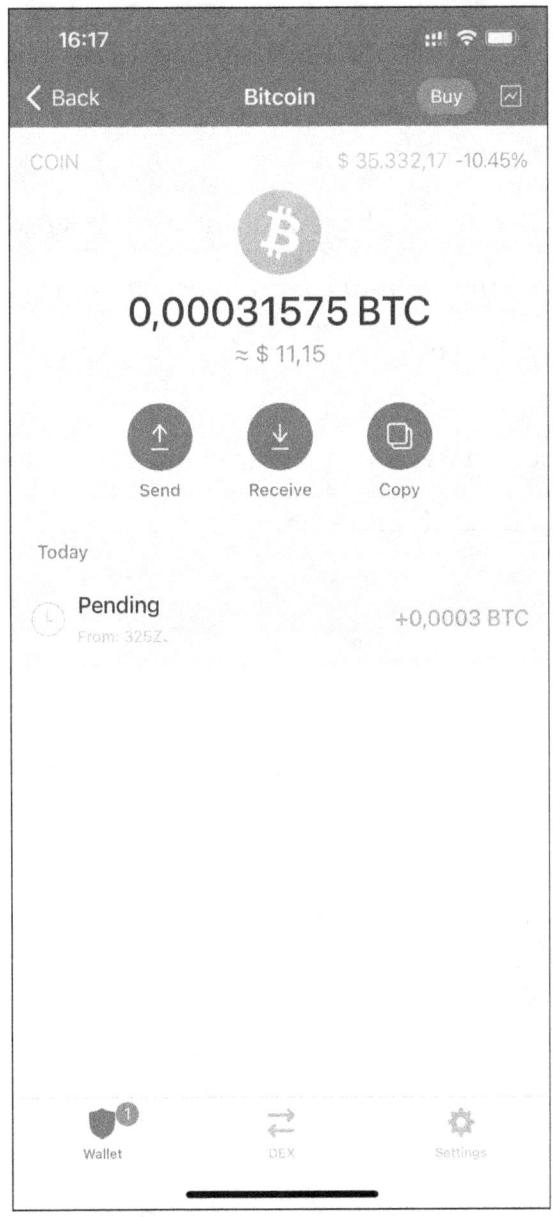

Figure 5.5 - Pending transaction

Here is one aspect of the management of Bitcoin that you will have to deal. All transactions take time to confirm. As you can see from Figure 5.6, my transaction appears as "Pending." What does it mean? We are still waiting for confirmation from the network to verify if the sender has funds.

Remember that a wallet doesn't have any Bitcoins; instead, it has a Private Key that controls a certain amount of funds in the Blockchain. The network verifies if the Private Key provided by the exchange wallet has the coins and confirm the process.

By taping at the wallet transaction, you can view more details about the process and the missing conformations (Figure 5.6).

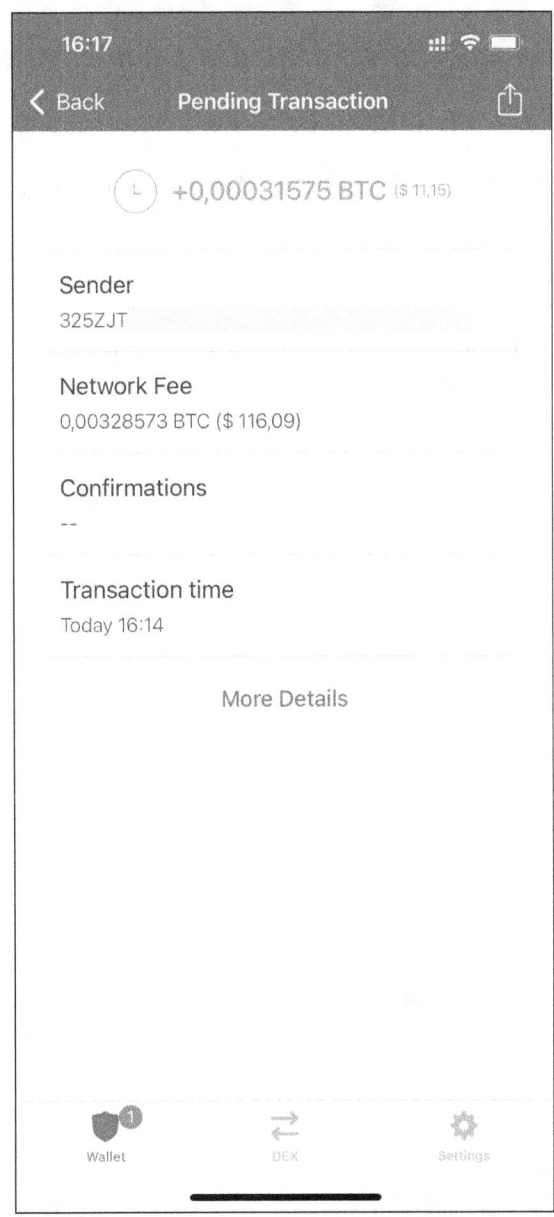

Figure 5.6 - Transaction details

How much time do you have to wait? It depends on several factors, and network congestion is one huge aspect of the required time.

For this particular transaction, I had to wait 25 minutes to get a total of 15 confirmations. That means 15 different nodes from the Bitcoin network confirmed that the exchange Private Key successfully signed the transaction and has the necessary funds (Figure 5.7).

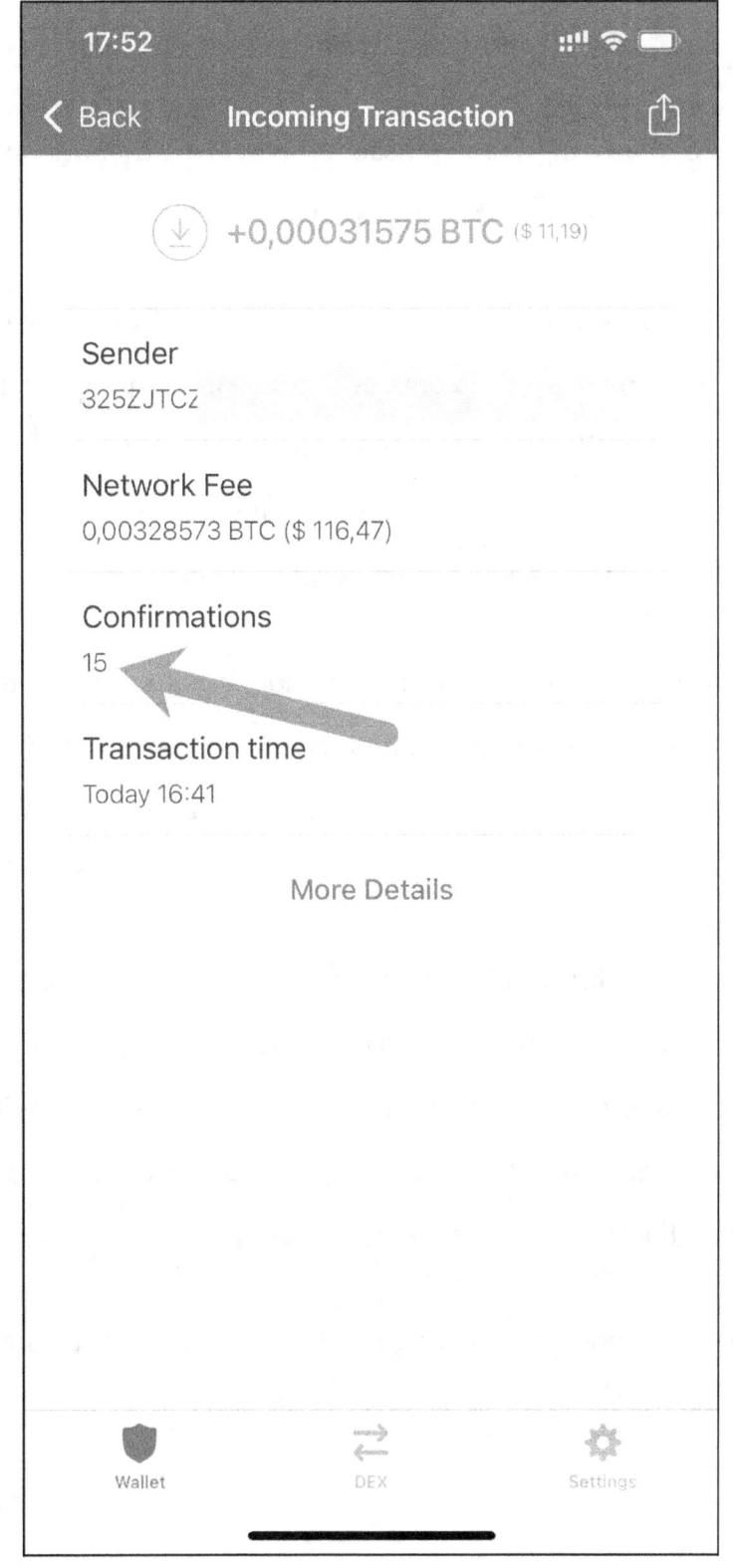

Figure 5.7 - *15 confirmations*

Usually, it is safe to assume your transaction is real with about six confirmations and the funds are in your wallet. It is now an irreversible transaction.

The entire process is secure and reliable, but it is at the same time one of the most frustrating aspects of managing Bitcoins and a reason for people not to accept the coins as payment in retail. With such long confirmation times, you can imagine yourself in line to buy groceries and, after sending the funds to the store wallet, moving to the side to way for all necessary confirmations.

If you decide to use a regular payment method like cash or a credit card, your confirmation for that transaction is instantaneous. You can swipe the card, and the bank tells the merchant if they approve or not the transaction. With Bitcoin, you must receive a few confirmations to ensure the funds are in your wallet.

Why should you wait for at least six confirmations? The primary reason to wait for so many confirmations is to avoid the double-spending problem. Moving funds from an exchange to yourself is safe, and the exchange system will prevent you from sending the same funds twice. However, nothing might stop someone else from trying to send the same funds to two different people.

When that happens, you must wait for the network to process and handle the transfer. If someone tries to send the same funds twice:

1. The network might give you one confirmation for both of the transactions

2. Starting with the second confirmation, one of them will confirm, and the second one probably gets rejected

3. With a third confirmation, you start to see one of the transactions receiving sequential approvals

4. The other transaction keeps showing as rejected. As a result, it won't go to the Bitcoin ledger

Since getting multiple confirmations is the only way to ensure you received the funds, you should wait at least for six of them. It is even more important when receiving funds from someone else other than yourself!

Info: other cryptocurrencies are offering much faster confirmation times when making transactions. For instance, when compared to Bitcoin, we have much shorter times to wait when using Ethereum you can get 20 confirmations in about 5 minutes.

5.3 Bitcoin fees

How do you feel about banking fees? We could easily live without that was a choice, but unfortunately, we have to pay them. If you are trying to use Bitcoin, or other cryptocurrencies, to move assets between wallets, you will also have to pay fees.

Before I explain how Bitcoin fees work, it is important to remember how the system works to clarify that those fees are different from those you pay to a bank.

The Bitcoin network and Blockchain are decentralized and work with computers, called Nodes, located worldwide. In fact, with the proper hardware and a reliable internet connection, you can join this network. The people keeping those computers connected to the network, with a node, receive the name of miners.

A miner is an important part of the Blockchain because they provide all computational power required to verify transactions. They keep everything working and ensure only signed transactions are valid. To verify each transaction, a miner must perform a series of complex math calculations on his computer and validate a transaction.

Stop for a moment to think about what a miner has to do:

– Get a powerful computer

– Keep it connected to the network

– Validate other people transactions

Will he or she do that for free? No, I believe that no one would keep that running for a long time without any compensation. That is why all transactions in the Bitcoin network has a fee. The fee is part of what keeps the wheel spinning and makes the Bitcoin network alive.

Those are different fees from the ones you pay at an exchange. If you open the wallet app and try to send coins to another person, you will also see a fee subtracted from the transaction. A software wallet includes the appropriate fee for you in the transaction (Figure 5.8).

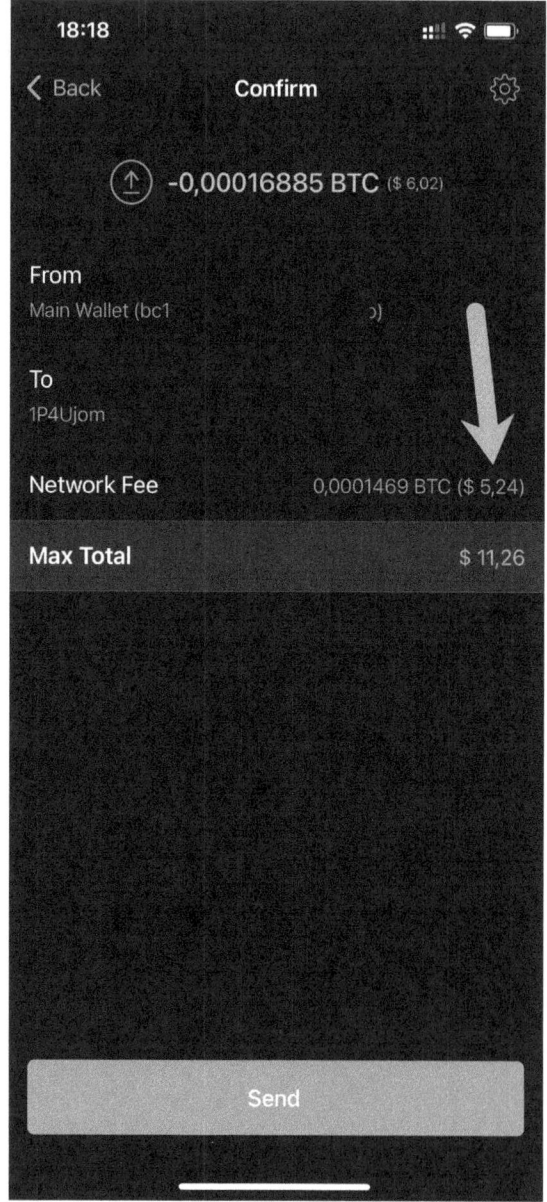

Figure 5.8 - Wallet fee

The fee in a Bitcoin transaction is important and can become critical when doing transactions requiring fast confirmations. Here are a few details about Bitcoin fees:

– The fee goes entirely to the miner

– The sender is responsible for paying the fee

– You can adjust the fee to "control" confirmation speeds

Why the fee has a direct impact on confirmation speeds? Because with higher fees, you have a better chance of having a miner to picking your transaction and process it faster.

Info: Most software wallets give you an estimate about an optimal fee to get a fast transaction.

5.3.1 Transaction size

Every transaction in the Bitcoin network must consider the entire ledger for processing purposes. As we mentioned before, all coins stay at the Blockchain, and you don't currently store any of them in a wallet. The wallet keeps the Private Keys safe, which gives you control over that balance.

Since the coins remain in the Blockchain, a transaction must do a series of calculations and checks to verify the balance.

For instance, imagine that two people sent you Bitcoins:

– Ana sent you 0,3 BTC

– Bob sent you 0,7 BTC

Your wallet now has a balance of 1 BTC. After receiving those transactions, the Bitcoin ledger will do the math for you, and the Private Key associated with your wallet now controls 1 BTC.

What if you decide to send 0,85 BTC to Alice? You can get Alice's Public Address and send her the funds. Now, to send that amount, the network verifies the history behind each part of the Bitcoins:

1. Starting with Ana and Bob

2. Their transfer of funds to your wallet

3. Your transfer to Alice

If Ana and Bob received Bitcoins from other people, the network would also track them. This history creates a small amount of data that goes to the Bitcoin network.

Each transaction on the Bitcoin network has a size measured in bytes with the digital signature and information about the funds' history.

5.3.2 Block size

Part of a miner's work is to process a piece of Block in the Bitcoin network. The current limit today is 1,000,000 bytes (1 megabyte) per block. For instance, a block is a sum of multiple transactions that fill up all space available until it reaches the limit.

Once they have the block ready, it is time to do all the complicated math and validate them.

In the first versions of Bitcoin, that limit was 32,000,000 bytes (32 megabytes), but Satoshi changed the code to reduce the block size.

5.3.3 The unconfirmed transaction pool

Back in our example, when you try to send 0,85 BTC to Alice, the total size of that transaction could be something like 250 bytes. That is a small size when you think about data only. How does the network calculate the fees? For each transaction, you will pay a certain amount of satoshi, which is the lowest division of a Bitcoin 0,00000001 BTC per byte.

For instance, if you pay 20 satoshi per each byte:

– **Transaction size:** 250 bytes

– **Fee rate:** 20 satoshi / byte

– **Total fee:** (20*0,00000001*250) → *0,00005 BTC*

The fee doesn't take into consideration the number of coins sent in a transaction. What matters here is the transaction size. It could be 100 BTC or 1 BTC. You would pay the same fee.

To get the exact cost of a transaction, you must take into consideration several factors like:

Network congestion

Size in bytes

From a miner's point of view, a transaction with a higher fee per byte is more profitable. As a result, it has a much better chance of being picked for processing. If you were a miner yourself, I believe that it would be an easy rule to follow. Only pick transactions that can maximize your profits.

Once you hit the send in a wallet, the data goes to an unconfirmed pool with other transactions, waiting for a miner to grab it for processing. By default, a transaction can stay in the pool for up to 72 hours, but it rarely stays that long. Once a miner picks it up for processing, it will send the confirmation to the Bitcoin ledger, and other miners will also contribute to the process.

5.3.4 SegWit transactions

A way of reducing fees for transactions in the Bitcoin network is to use the Segregated Witness (SegWit) protocol. How to use that type of transaction? Pick a wallet that accepts transactions using a Public Key with the protocol. If you remember from our explanation about Public keys in Bitcoin, a wallet address could start with a "1":

```
Public key example:
```

With a SegWit compatible address, you have it starting with "bc1":

```
SegWit address:
```

Should you use wallets supporting this protocol? Sure! It means you will pay fewer fees for moving the balance.

5.3.5 Changing the fee

How can you set the fees for a particular transaction? Depending on the wallet you are using to interact with the Blockchain, you can edit the fee you wish to pay manually. If you don't want to change that, a wallet software usually picks an optimal value.

But, you can always go to the wallet settings (Figure 5.9).

Figure 5.9 - Wallet settings

There you can set the fee rate you wish to pay (Figure 5.10).

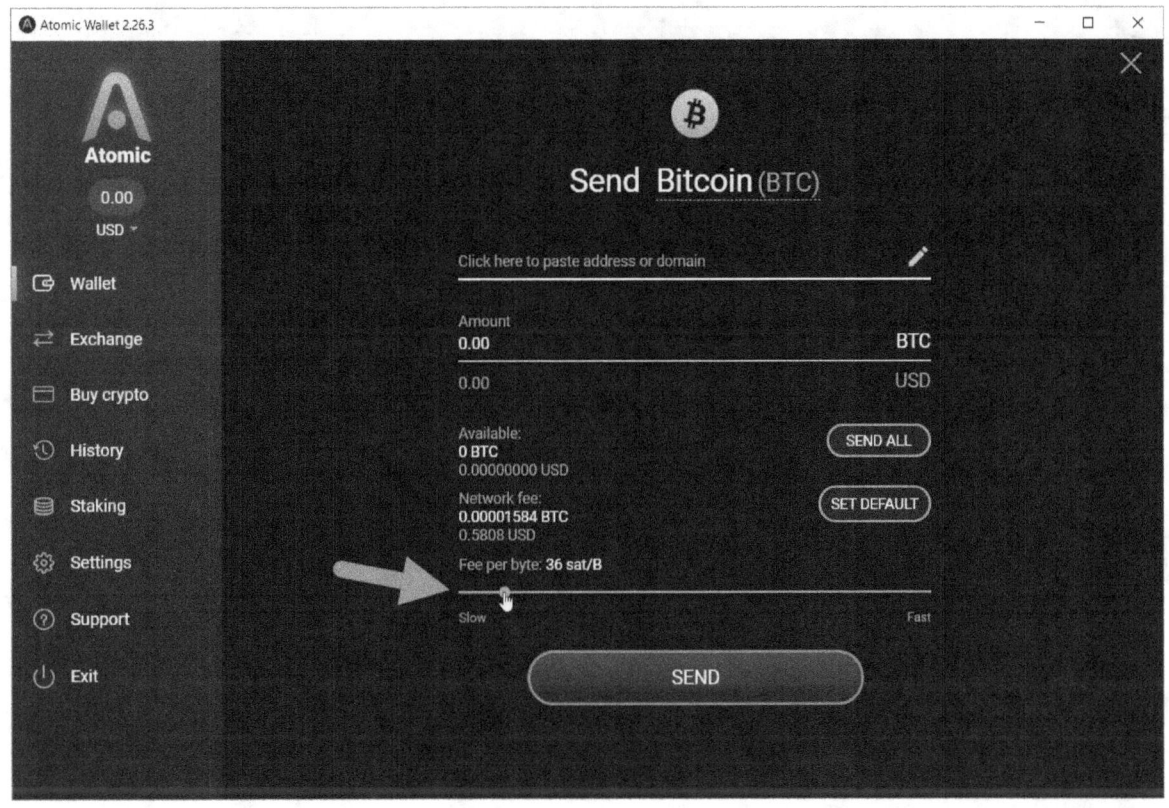

Figure 5.10 - *Changing the fee rate*

One thing to keep in mind is that confirmation speed and cost depends on several factors:

– Network congestion

– Fee paid to the miner

– Size of your transaction

What happens if you pay a fee that is below average? That means you will have to wait for long periods until a miner picks your transaction. When making transfers between wallets your wallets, you can set a low fee. Unless you need the funds transferred quickly, you can set a low fee and wait a couple of hours for confirmation and save some Bitcoins.

Since network congestion is a huge factor, you can expect the average fee cost to fluctuate. Some sites try to estimate the current cost and time required for processing:

– https://bitcoiner.live/

– https://bitcoinfees.net/

– https://mempool.space/

Those are estimates only, and you should use them as a reference if you wish to change the cost for each transaction manually.

5.4 How to cancel a transaction?

Is it possible to cancel a transaction you send with Bitcoins? Like we mentioned before, after you receive a confirmation and it is in the Bitcoin ledger, your transaction is irreversible. But, there is a way of speeding up a transaction.

Before I explain how it works, let me state that it involves risk and will cost you higher fees.

Here is what some people do when they need to speed up a transaction:

1. Imagine that you transferred funds to another wallet, and since you are not in a hurry, the fees were set to a bare minimum.

2. After a couple of hours, you realize that you need the funds faster.

3. The procedure, in this case, is to start a new transfer using the same amount but significantly increasing the fee. A transaction with a low fee might stay for a long time in the unconfirmed pool waiting for the miner.

4. Once you send the same amount with a higher fee, it is very likely that a miner will pick it up immediately.

5. After the transaction with the highest fee receives a confirmation; the network will automatically reject the other transaction with a low fee.

Isn't it double-spending? It is an attempt of double-spending that gets rejected. That is why you should avoid it at all costs, and some wallets don't even let you do the operation.

Other than that, you can't cancel a transaction. The only thing you can do is speed up the process.

What is next?

Many people who start to manage and trade Bitcoins discover the role of miners in the network and wonder if they could also start to make money by becoming one. Is that a profitable operation? It might give you some profit, but that depends on several factors.

The next chapter discusses the role and details about the requirements to start a mining business and if you should invest in such an operation.

We also go more in-depth into using an exchange to trade Bitcoins and discuss the substantial price fluctuations of the cryptocurrency.

Chapter 6 - Earning and trading Bitcoins

A question that many people starting with Bitcoin has is how to get the coins? At this point, you already have a wallet or multiple of them with no control over Bitcoins. Our objective in this chapter is to give you some of the best options regarding acquiring the coins.

Would you like to try mining Bitcoins? Even though some people think mining is a way of getting free Bitcoins, there are many mining costs. If you don't plan carefully, you will not get a profit.

The second half focuses on exchanges and how you can use them for trading Bitcoins and strategies to reduce your risk when using their services.

Here is a list of what you will learn:

– How mining works?

– Should you start mining?

– Is it possible to make money mining?

– Using an exchange

– What is the KYC initiative?

– The risks of using an exchange

6.1 Earning Bitcoins (Mining)

In the previous chapter, we discussed a key role in the Bitcoin network, responsible for validating and confirm transactions from people sending funds to a new address. The miners have a key role in the network and are part of what makes Bitcoin a democratic Blockchain solution. Each miner has a node of the network and contributes to the decentralization of Bitcoin.

How do they do that? The process to become a miner is simple, and as we mentioned before, you can easily download the software (Bitcoin core) and join the network today as a miner. Before you download anything, I strongly advise you to read the first part of this chapter to make up your mind about mining.

By the way, you can download Bitcoin core from this address:

```
https://bitcoin.org
```

To become a miner, you need the software to interact with the Bitcoin network and a powerful computer to perform all the complex math behind mining blocks. How much computer power do we need for mining?

What if I told you that you could mine a few hundred Bitcoins a month with an old computer? That was true back in 2010 and 2011, when mining was easy. Back there, you could get an average laptop and connect it to the network and earn a few hundred Bitcoins.

Info: The first block mined by Satoshi Nakamoto himself gave him a reward of 50 BTC. At the time, it was worthless, but today it has a value of 1,8 Million USD.

Was Bitcoin popular in 2009? Not at all, and only a few people supported the network as miners. It was already a revolutionary project, but it took a while to gain traction as a way to store value. In May of 2010, we had the incredible price of 0,01 USD for 1 BTC. Only in 2011, the price of a Bitcoin reached 1 USD.

Would you leave your computer running 24 hours for a project that had a value of 0.01 USD per unit? Only a few enthusiasts jumped into mining, and if they kept the coins until today, you could imagine how happy they must be.

After a couple of years, the mining process got harder, and old computers could not handle the intense computational tasks. By design, the mining process of Bitcoin requires more computational power over time.

One of the reasons to control Bitcoin rewards for mining is to keep the supply of coins low.

6.1.1 Mining hardware

A computer that has the purpose of mining Bitcoin must have a strong CPU (*central processing unit*), and for a long time, that was all you needed to start. When those CPUs were struggling to deliver optimal performance, the task went to modern GPUs (*graphical processing units*) that gave incredible results when used to mine.

With a good GPU used for 3D games, we could mine Bitcoins with a reasonable return. At some point, it even caused a shortage of those parts for general consumers because miners were buying them in bulk to create mining farms.

Today it is more likely to find miners using specialized hardware to mine Bitcoin and solve the complex math behind it. That is because not even some of the most powerful GPUs can handle the processing power anymore.

Since Bitcoin mining became a way for many people and companies to make money, some specialized computers appeared to give miners only what they need. That is when the ASIC computers appeared. It stands for *Application Specific Integrated Circuits* and it is a computer with a single purpose only: mine Bitcoins. It doesn't have any other function.

Info: The Bitcoin mining difficulty keeps adjusting itself to ensure a new block appears around 10 minutes. After mining creates 2,016 blocks (about 14 days), the system changes the difficulty level.

6.2 Can you make money with mining?

A question that many people starting to manage Bitcoins ask themselves is where they should start mining? Can you make money by becoming a miner? Sure, it is possible to earn a lot of Bitcoins from mining. But, you should consider several factors before starting to mining Bitcoins.

To mine Bitcoins, you need:

- Specialised hardware

- Reliable internet connection

- Software to set up a node

A key element of the mining process is power consumption. Cryptocurrency mining involves complex math can bring any system to its limits. Since the computer must use 100% of its processing capabilities uninterruptedly, you will have a significant power consumption and, therefore, a huge bill.

For that reason, a lot of miners choose to build their mining rigs in locations with cheap electricity. Remember the mining, to be profitable, requires from you some managing skills. It works like a business where you have to balance costs and gains.

Besides the power bill, you also have to pick a location to create a mining farm, a place with multiple computers connected in a local network. Do you need multiple computers? If you consider that a single computer can return around 5 USD per day, it is easy to assume one device alone won't help you grow a mining business.

You need more computers to create a sustainable business in mining. That is why many miners set up a mining farm.

Those mining farms can give you some extra work:

– **Maintenance:** With so many computers running in the same location, it is inevitable that you have to replace and service them eventually.

– **Network:** To create an effective farm of computers, you need to set up a local network and provide maintenance.

– **Cooling:** Having so many computers running at full speed in a closed space generates a lot of heat. You must find a way to cool down the environment and ensure they don't suffer a performance loss.

With that in mind, you can start deciding if mining is a good solution for your needs. What is the most important factor? The cost of electricity is by far what defines if a mining farm can give profits.

There are even some tools that calculate your estimated profits based on several factors:

```
https://btc.com/tools/mining-calculator
```

The calculator also includes the cost of each KWh. You can fill the numbers based on the cost where you live to find if you can profit from mining.

If you decide to invest in mining, an alternative is to join a mining pool. This is a group of computers that share their computational capacity to act as a super processor. It results in faster mining speeds, and after the pool mines a Bitcoin, they share the results.

As a beginner, should you invest in mining? If you are starting with cryptocurrencies, I advise you to stay away from mining unless you like to handle the technical aspects of managing multiple computers and network settings.

6.2.1 Investing in mining hardware

What if you decide to jump into mining anyway? In that case, I recommend you to look for specialized types of computers for that purpose. The best solutions for mining today are ASIC devices. It is an acronym for *application-specific integrated circuit*. It is a computer that has a single purpose; mining.

There are multiple options available, with prices going from 2,500 USD to 15,000 USD. What makes them so expansive? The measure that you need to look at in those devices is the speed given in *Tera Hashes per second* (Th/s).

A high value in *Tera Hashes per second* means the mining device is more efficient. As a result, it will become more profitable and valuable.

6.2.2 Mining around the world

The decentralized nature of Bitcoin is one of the strongest aspects of the currency and what makes it impossible to "shut down." Anyone with an internet connection can join the network and create a new node.

Those nodes might come from a single person that transformed a room in his house into a mining farm or from companies that rent warehouses full of ASIC devices, creating a massive mining farm. We can find those warehouses in locations with cold weather and cheap electricity.

Some popular locations with massive mining farms are in northern China and Iceland.

Starting a mining business might give you some trouble in certain regions worldwide because it is illegal to trade cryptocurrencies or environmental factors. For instance, you won't find much mining activity in hot or warm locations. You would have to pay a lot for both electricity and cooling.

6.3 Buying and selling from an exchange

The option of earning Bitcoins with mining is not the best solution for many people due to the technical requirements of purchasing and keeping a mining facility. When entering the cryptocurrency ecosystem, the easiest and fastest solution to get coins is to buy from someone else.

Do you know anyone interested in selling Bitcoins? It is not good to go to the street and start asking people to sell their Bitcoins.

To make your life easier and connect people interested in trading Bitcoins, we have exchanges. Those are places where anyone can buy or sell cryptocurrency using multiple types of payment.

With a cryptocurrency exchange, you find a location where people that hold Bitcoins, and other cryptocurrencies, use to trade their assets. There are two main types of exchanges:

– Custodian based centralized exchanges

– Non-custodian decentralized exchanges

The easiest type for beginners is the first one, which is a custodian based centralized exchanges. It gets this name because you must send your Bitcoins to their exchange wallet for trading, and they can hold the balance for your convenience. Usually, this type of exchange has a company behind with centralized control and management.

How do they work? A typical workflow for using such exchanges would be:

1. Fund the account with fiat currency (Bank transfer or debit card)

2. Place an order to buy Bitcoins with that balance

3. The exchange connects you with someone trying to sell Bitcoins

4. You receive the Bitcoin in your web-based wallet

Later, you can also use the exchange to cash out the Bitcoin. You can place an order to sell your coins and receive fiat currency (Dollars, Euros, or other). From the balance in your exchange, you can withdraw that to your bank account.

Of course, in several exchanges, you have to pay small fees for every type of transaction. This is a major factor in picking an exchange. Make sure you research before starting to use such a service.

What about non-custodian decentralized exchanges? Those types of exchanges give you a way to connect to other traders directly. You avoid the fee from a custodian exchange and take control over the entire process. Depending on the person you are trading with, it is possible to use multiple payment types not available in centralized exchanges.

For instance, a person trading Bitcoins can accept PayPal or other payment means only available in certain regions.

If you are a beginner and never had the opportunity to trade cryptocurrencies start with custodian based centralized exchanges. They offer the easiest and reliable way of trading Bitcoins.

Info: Those decentralized exchanges also receive a name of DEX.

6.3.1 The KYC regulations

Before you jump into an exchange to start trading, you should be aware of a regulation that serious exchanges must follow. They will ask you for proof of documentation and other documents after registering. It is part of the KYC (Known your customer) effort to minimize the risk of fraud and criminal actives in exchanges.

If you create an account and receive a request to send copies of documents and even taking a selfie with your phone, it is typical verification to allow people to trade.

For transactions involving credit and debit cards, the exchange might ask you additional details about the card. Since transactions with Bitcoin are irreversible, any fraud with such cards might cause huge losses for the exchange itself, and they must ensure you are the person behind the purchase.

6.3.2 How to choose an exchange?

When looking for an exchange to buy or sell Bitcoins, you will quickly notice something about them. There are thousands of exchanges around the world trading cryptocurrencies. All of them offer a unique range of features and options depending on where you live.

When choosing an exchange, you must keep an eye on trading fees and how easy it is to deposit and withdraw money from your wallet. Using bank transfers is the cheapest way of funding your account.

For instance, if you live in the United States, some local exchanges make it easy to trade crypto with an ACH bank transfer. Other exchanges based in Europe work better with local banks.

Info: Avoid using a credit card to buy Bitcoins unless you have no other option. The reason to not use a credit card is due to incredibly high fees. Some exchanges can charge you close to 10% in fees when using a credit card.

What are the best options regarding centralized custodian base exchanges? Here are some of the largest exchanges operating today:

1. Binance

2. Coinbase Pro

3. Kraken

Those are only a few of them, and you should look for an option that suits your needs when trading Bitcoins. Nowadays, the largest exchange in the world is Binance. Both in trading volume and active users. They even offer different branches for certain locations. For instance, there is *Binance* exchange and *Binance US* exchange. The US version works better for United States residents.

Besides availability and fees, you should also look for additional details about an exchange like:

– Trading limits

– Mobile app option

– How much cryptocurrency you can trade

– Withdraws in cash

– Additional trading features (API)

The trading limits can get into the way of people trying to get large volumes of Bitcoin or withdraw a substantial amount to a bank account. In some cases, an exchange can hold your money for a couple of days before sending it to your bank.

What about fees? When might they charge a fee? Here are some types of transactions that can result in a fee:

– **Loading your wallet with fiat currency:** Sending money to your wallet balance using a credit card usually has the highest fee. Always try to use a bank deposit.

– **Trading Bitcoins:** When you buy or sell Bitcoins in an exchange, they will subtract a small fee. That also valid for other cryptocurrencies.

– **Withdraws:** A withdrawal of crypto to an external wallet or in fiat currency also results in a fee.

Each exchange has unique fees for those types of operations, and you should search and each one of them to find the best option for your needs.

You should also look for limits regarding trading. For instance, imagine that you found an old Private Key that controls a wallet that has 100 BTC. You discover that you have 3,400,000.00 USD in the wallet! Can you send it to an exchange to sell everything at once? Most exchanges will allow you to send the entire Bitcoin balance to their wallets, but they might impose a limit on how much you can withdraw in cash.

Depending on the exchange, you might have limits like 50,000.00 USD a day for withdraws, which will delay your dream of having a millionaire balance in the bank.

Info: If you prefer decentralized exchanges, you should look to options like "Bisq", "Dydx", and "Uniswap."

6.3.3 Strategy to use an exchange

Can you start investing in Bitcoins or cryptocurrencies with no involvement in an exchange? Unless you decide to join the network as a miner, you will likely need to register in an exchange for trading. Otherwise, how will you get Bitcoins? Since an exchange is not risk-free, it is the perfect moment to present a strategy for using an exchange.

Suppose your plans involve acquiring Bitcoins to store value for savings, retirement, or anything in the long term. In that case, I recommend you to follow a simple procedure, which is using the exchange only for simple trading. Go there to buy coins and move them to cold storage as fast as possible.

Info: *When you use an exchange for buying and selling coins, it has the name of spot trading.*

For the cases when you make small investments monthly, you can keep small amounts there to save on withdrawal fees, but you will always be at risk:

```
Use the exchange for trading only. Never leave funds there
in the long term.
```

Is there any moment where people should keep funds in an exchange wallet? Yes, in some cases, it makes sense to use the web-based wallet. For instance, some people with more experience can try to day-trade with cryptocurrencies. In this case, it is natural to keep the funds in the wallet.

Since day trading demands funds for buying and selling for profit, you need the liquidity for that particular type of move. Is day trading possible with cryptocurrencies? Absolutely! There are even Bots that can help you trade coins non-stop.

What is a Bot? It is software that can do the trading for you based on rules you define.

They offer you an automated to try a profit with price fluctuations. Is it suitable for beginners? Unless you feel comfortable leaving the funds under the control of software, it is a wise decision to hire someone to do that for you.

As a beginner, you should try spot trading first. When you understand the market and trading tools, you can move to more advanced and more risky trading options.

6.3.4 The risks of using an exchange (Privacy)

One of the advantages of using Bitcoins and cryptocurrencies, in general, is the enhanced privacy regarding your financial life. As you could notice from our multiple explanations about wallets and Public addresses, it is impossible to link a wallet to a person or entity. You might know the Public address, but the owner of that wallet remains unknown.

A digital wallet's address might easily become traceable when using an exchange due to a Blockchain explorer. As protection from possible liabilities of people trading Bitcoins for illegal purposes like money laundry and tax evasion, most exchanges require identity verification to trade Bitcoins. That is part of the KYC initiative.

Some of them might require:

– Photo ID (Drivers license or Passport)

– Selfie

– Proof of address

That means an exchange can expose your data if they receive something like a court order. When they expose your data to law enforcement, it will be possible to connect your identity to all wallet addresses that interact with your account.

If you only want to buy Bitcoins as an investment and keep paying your taxes, it shouldn't be a problem. But, if privacy is a concern for you, an exchange that doesn't require verification is the best option.

Info: Is there a truly private cryptocurrency? One of the best options regarding privacy today is Monero (XMR). They use temporary Public addresses for each transaction.

6.3.5 What if an exchange gets hacked or go out of business?

From all the possible risks involved in using an exchange, the possibility of a hack or financial insolvency is among the highest. A hack is when someone or a group of people can break into the exchange security and access the Private Keys. When something like that happens, the effects will usually be devastating. With a Private Key, it will be possible to transfer all the Bitcoins from the exchange.

It usually means all funds from wallets are lost forever. If you use an exchange and keep the Bitcoin balance there, it is at risk of being hacked. It happened in the past and will probably happen again.

Some exchanges do not disclose how they secure the Private Keys from their wallets, and it is a liability. If you keep a balance in such an exchange, it is a good idea to withdraw them as soon you finish trading.

If you look at each exchange's features, you will find that some are more transparent about managing Private Keys. For instance, they may have the keys in cold storage and even documents for their customers. It means that a possible hack won't have access to the Bitcoin balance. Those are the most secure types of exchanges.

Another possibility that always frightens people with funds in an exchange is the company go out of business.

There are signs point to possible trouble with an exchange. An immediate red flag is a delay in withdraws or problems transferring funds to external wallets.

6.3.6 The Mt. Gox case

To demonstrate how dangerous it is to keep a balance in a web-based wallet, we can tell the history of one of the most famous hacks related to Bitcoin and an exchange. Have you ever heard of a company called Mt. Gox?

In 2014, there were much fewer options to exchange Bitcoins online, and one of them had a significant presence in the community. Japan-based Mt. Gox had a massive trading volume in Bitcoin. The company started doing business in 2010 and skyrocket to become the largest marketplace to buy and sell Bitcoins in 2014.

It had an incredible 70% of the market share! Due to the volume and popularity of Bitcoin today, it would be difficult to achieve the same volume.

What happened to them? In early 2014 the company suddenly halted all operations related to Bitcoin trading and closed its website. It was a shocking move for a lot of traders at the time.

A few weeks later, they announced that 850,000 BTC disappeared from their wallets. A hacker had access to the Private Keys in their system and transferred that incredible amount of coins. An investigation later discovered that those coins started to move out of their wallets in 2011, always in small transactions.

Anyone with Bitcoins in their wallet at Mt. Gox lost their balance. Some people are trying to recover their losses with legal actions, but it is very unlikely that they will get anything back. The price of Bitcoins at the time was around 400 USD. If you had 10 BTC (4,000 USD), they would have to pay you back around 350,000 USD today.

It is a lesson about the liabilities of keeping a balance for longer periods in an exchange. Unless you have a blind trust in the way they handle security, it is not a good idea to leave your funds there. For long-term investments, it is always better to invest in cold storage like a hardware wallet.

That way, you ensure maximum security to store your Private Keys.

What is next?

Are you ready to start buying Bitcoins and become part of the Blockchain revolution? At this point in the book, you have all information necessary to start trading and store value with Bitcoins. However, we can add a few more details about how to secure your assets.

With new markets like cryptocurrencies, there is always a potential risk from price fluctuations and security. It is common to find people trying to take advantage of their features, and criminals and scammers love cryptocurrencies. Why? Because it is private and irreversible. Once they get your Bitcoin, it is impossible to recover.

For that reason, we will discuss what measures you can take to enhance and safeguard your Bitcoins in the next chapter.

Chapter 7 - How to safeguard Bitcoins

The world of cryptocurrencies has a considerable potential to bring financial independence to many people, but it also has many risks. It is a playground for scammers and hackers trying to gain control of your precious Bitcoins, and you must take measurements to ensure nothing happens to your balance.

Besides the usual dangers of a computer system connected to the internet, we also have failed backups and missing recovery keys. When something like that happens, you are at risk of losing access to your Bitcoins.

The following chapter offers several tips and recommendations about how you can enhance your cryptocurrencies' security and create a plan to recover a wallet if something goes wrong.

Here is a list of what you will learn:

– The Bitcoin security

– Private Keys and recovery phrases importance

– The weal link in Bitcoin security

– How to create a recovery plan

– Planning for your heirs

7.1 The Bitcoin Security

The current supply of available Bitcoins today is somewhere around 18,5 Million BTC available in the Blockchain. That is a lot of coins around for people looking to invest or save money using cryptocurrencies. As we already mentioned before, none of those coins goes to a wallet. They all remain in the Blockchain.

A wallet has the primary purpose of storing the Private Key, which can control a balance and give access to send Bitcoins to another address.

What if I told you that about 20% of those 18,5 million coins are lost forever? That is close to 3,7 million BTC no one can claim or use. They are in wallets where their owners either lost or forget the Private Keys with no means to recover them.

How much those 3,7 million BTC worth today? About 120 Billion USD lost forever!

Unless you want to join those who are mourning today because they lost one of the most valuable assets nowadays, you must start to take your backup procedure and security as seriously as possible.

I read a disturbing story in an online forum about Bitcoin of a person looking to recover their funds. In 2011, he tried that new thing called Bitcoin and mine about 120 BTC to a wallet. Since Bitcoins worth very little at the time, he didn't make any backup of the Private Keys.

Info: In the early days of Bitcoin, you could get mining rewards of 20 BTC to 30 BTC in a single day of mining.

He was 18 back in 2011, and today he has a family and lots of debts to cover and no job because of the pandemic. He has this wallet with 120 BTC with almost 4 Million USD, which he can't use. Is there a way to recover it? Can he call anybody? No, unfortunately, he must find a way to recover the Private Keys.

That is a terrifying feeling to know that in such difficult times with a family to care for and no job, you have 4 million USD in a wallet that you can't use.

Because of Blockchain's strong security with cryptography, it is nearly impossible to recover a Private Key if you don't have a backup. The same applies to the 12-word recovery Phrase from software wallets.

Unless you don't want to contribute to this enormous amount of lost money, I strongly suggest you start taking measures to safeguard your Bitcoins. This involves making secure backups and a small system to recover them in case anything happens.

7.2 Private keys and recovery phrases

For people that are not familiar with technology and how computers work, the concept of a Blockchain and a cryptocurrency wallet is odd. It has the name of wallet, but it doesn't hold any money, just a long and weird code that controls digital money spread in computers worldwide.

Understand that concept is a key part of engaging in this data's backups because, unlike digital photos or PDFs, you can't print or copy Bitcoins to an external hard drive.

The only thing you possess that gives you control over Bitcoins is the Private Keys or seed phrase for your wallet. A wallet is a way to store and encapsulate Private Keys to give you a great security level.

Info: Some wallets call the recovery phrase as seed phrase. Regardless of the name, they work the same way.

We can easily say that instead of Bitcoins, your most valuable asset is the Private Key. If you lose it, you can't do anything with your Bitcoins. For that reason, you must create a plan to keep them safe and in multiple locations whenever possible.

Why multiple locations?

If you write it down on a piece of paper and keep it in your house, you must ensure that nothing might happen to that paper. Multiple events can destroy that piece of paper:

– Fire

– Hurricane

– Flood

– Dog

– Kids

Just to name a few of the natural disasters and events that can cause huge damage to a house and eventually destroy your physical copy of the Private Key or recovery phrase. In some cases, a dog or a child can do more damage to that paper than natural disasters. Make sure you keep the backup in a safe location!

With Bitcoin, you can be responsible for your financial life with all the benefits and liabilities.

Info: Why so many people keep recommending the use of a piece of paper as a backup to your Private Keys or seed phrases? It is simple; no one can hack a piece of paper. Unless you type it in a computer, a hacker doesn't have any way of stealing your funds other than getting the paper. This also includes taking a photo of your paper, which will put your balance at risk.

7.3 The weak link in the Blockchain

Let me tell you something that might become a huge surprise and is about the security of Bitcoin. There is a weak link in Bitcoin that most criminals and scammers try to explore. Do you want to know what it is? The security weakness is the owner of a wallet. Yes, the weakest link in most digital systems is the user.

You probably heard of many stories and news about a hacker that could breach a system's security and had access to private and classified information. In most cases, the hacker wasn't a technology mastermind with impressive skills and tools to crack military-grade security. He, or she, was only clever enough to take advantage of a lack of care or judgment from a system user.

For instance, a person with administrative access to a system could have a weak and easy to guess password. Have you ever heard of a person that wrote a password to a computer on a sticky note and placed it on the monitor? You will find many ways for people to put systems at risk because they are reckless about security.

Another terrible mistake made by people is to reuse passwords. Do you have the same password for your e-mail? Computer? Bank account? Bitcoin exchange?

By doing that, you put your entire digital life at risk because by finding one password for your accounts, a potential "hacker" can gain access to all of our accounts.

Of course, if you lose access to your e-mail, it is easy to recover. There is always support from the e-mail provider. But, it is not the case with a password from an exchange. If someone enters the account and transfer the funds, it is very unlikely that you will get it back.

It can get even worse in cases where you have an exchange with a linked bank account or credit card. The hacker can buy Bitcoins and withdraw them to his wallet. Since those transactions are irreversible, you will have to deal with the credit card company or bank to pay the bill.

Tip: A great way of staying safer online is using a password manager to create strong and unique passwords for each service and have up-to-date software.

7.3.1 They want your Private Keys

Since the Private Keys to a wallet are the most valuable asset in possession of a person investing in Bitcoins, the vast majority of scams related to the currency tries to make you disclose this precious information. A potential scammer can do that in many ways.

There are multiple cases where a scammer can try to get your Private Keys or seed phrases:

– **Fake wallet apps:** From time to time, we find fake apps that use similar names of popular mobile wallets. By downloading it to your brand new phone, you can enter the seed phrase to restore your wallet and grant scammer access to your funds.

– **Fake sites:** If you open the website of an exchange directly from a bookmark, it is unlikely that it will go to a malicious copy of that site. However, a lot of people still type the service in Google to open the site. A scammers technique is to buy ads in Google or Facebook to place a fake copy in search results or social media. If you don't pay attention, you might go to a phishing site, which will ask for your seed phrase.

– **Support calls or emails:** A scammer may find out that you have a hardware wallet from a leaked database and call or email you about a potential problem with the device. To help you solve the issue, he needs the recovery phrase.

Those are a few examples of cases where people will try to make you give away the Private Keys or recovery phrase for a wallet. You must always double-check if you are on the correct website or have a legitimate app before entering any sensitive information.

Even if you have a backup of the Private Keys or recovery phrase in a piece of paper, by typing it into a computer and giving it away to a scammer, you put all your balance at risk.

If someone asks for your recovery phrase, it is a scammer.

7.3.2 Beware of malware

A common problem related to computer systems security has the name of malware. Multiple types of malware can help a criminal to steal information from a computer system. For instance, you can install the software on your computer that keeps sending the browsing history to a remote server. It can also keep track of your computer clipboard to find useful information.

Info: *The clipboard keep everything you copy on a computer or phone.*

When I say computer system, you can picture both desktop computers, tablets, and phones. Are there risks related to Bitcoin? Sure, it is an incredible target for malware. Think about how easy it is to take control of a wallet with a Private Key.

A scammer can be anywhere in the world, and with a Private Key he, or she, can easily transfer the funds anywhere. Since it is irreversible, you don't have any way of tracking the person or get your money back.

For that reason, a lot of malware targets Private Keys and recovery phrases. How they do that? A common practice is to look in your computer for text files with a keyword or pattern that looks like a recovery phrase. A text file with random 12 words has a high chance to be a recovery phrase for a cryptocurrency wallet.

It also works for phones where malicious apps can scan the clipboard for anything that looks like a Private Key or recovery phrase. If it is on your computer or phone screen and has an internet connection, it is a risk.

How to avoid malware? Usually, simple measures can help you reduce the risk of having malware in your computer or phone:

– Always use up to date software

– Avoid installing software or apps from unknown sources

– Have an antivirus or malware protection

– Be suspicious of links sent by messages or social media

Since malware is a problem for anyone with a connected device to the internet, most people that take security to the maximum level only keep offline copies of their Private Keys and recovery phrases. Once you see them on the computer screen or phone, take a piece of paper and write them down. Never place them in a text file or screenshot.

Of course, never type that information on a site or give it away by phone or email. You will make the life of people trying to steal Bitcoins or cryptocurrencies a lot harder.

7.3.3 Don't become a target

What would you do if you had a huge balance in your bank account? Would you start to post on social media about it? I believe no one would start to spread the word about how much money you own because it could start to make the wrong people follow and track you around.

The same principle applies to Bitcoins and cryptocurrencies. If you decide to invest and save money in Bitcoin, you should choose carefully where to disclose such information. The reason is simple; you might become a target. Since getting Bitcoins from someone else is irreversible and you can't go to the police or call someone for help, it is a great way to have "easy money."

If you start accumulating a balance in Bitcoins, you should make sure only a handful of people you trust know that, like your companion or parents. I know that telling about it to friends might make you look like a financial expert, but you never know if they will share that information with the wrong person.

7.4 Create a recovery plan

After you start to save using Bitcoins and achieve a reasonable amount in cryptocurrencies, it will be time to start thinking about a recovery plan. The plan doesn't have anything to do with price fluctuations of Bitcoin but focus on countermeasures about the possible loss of your backups.

Having a backup is a great way to avoid losing data in computer systems, but one step that people usually forget is to test if the backup works. You think you have a viable backup in many cases because the software or system is "working," but once you try to recover data, it fails.

The same principle applies to Bitcoin and cryptocurrencies. Once you create the wallet and have the Private Keys or recovery phrase at hand, it is time to back up this data. Not one back, but at least two. If you can make three, it will be even better.

Of course, all copies must be in separate locations. Otherwise, losing one could mean having all other copies compromised.

By far, the safest way of keeping them is in a location not connected to the internet. A piece of paper, as always, is a great way to make it private and "hacker free." However, you have to remember where you keep that paper and have a system to use it.

For instance, you can make copies of that paper:

– Hide the paper in a place only you know about

– Use some kind of vault in your home to keep it safe

– For large balances in Bitcoin, it might worth getting a safe deposit box in a bank

The key here is to find a place that only you know to hide the backup.

Try to laminate the paper to make it more resistant to water and tear. Get the equipment to laminate the copies yourself and not handle the paper to a third party.

How to test if the backup works? A simple way of making a test to see if the backup works is to set up a new wallet app from your phone or computer. Install it once again and type the recovery phrase. That will ensure you have a working phrase.

Before you try this backup recovery, it is important to keep only a small balance in the wallet. As low as possible for testing purposes. Only after you know that your backup system works start to send more coins to that wallet.

What about a hardware wallet? In case you decide to go with a hardware wallet, which is by far the safest way of keeping the Private Keys secure, you should follow the procedures described by the wallet manufacturer to test.

7.5 Heirs

Any long term investment in cryptocurrencies can bring huge gains for the holder of those tokens because the gains can easily surpass all other financial investments. You can take a glimpse of that by looking at historical data and see how much people gained after investing in Bitcoin for a couple of years.

That is great when you are trying to save money to cash out later. Getting ready for the future includes storing the Private Keys or recovery phrase for your wallet in a secure location and the recovery plan for when things go wrong.

It is incredible how people overlook the security and recovery plans for anything digital. That is probably because you can always use options from service providers to recover control of an account.

- **Did you forget the password to your email?** Use the recovery options provided by the service.

– **Forget the PIN to your credit card?** Call customer service, and they will update it for you.

With Bitcoin and cryptocurrency wallets, it doesn't work this way, and if you lose your Private Keys or phrase to the wallet, you also won't have access to the money.

In the previous section, we discussed creating a recovery plan, which tries to make a quick and reliable plan for your o regain access to the funds if you lost the device with either a software or hardware wallet.

One aspect of that backup that many people forget is ensuring your heirs know about them. Do you have children? A companion that must know about Bitcoin in case something happens to you? Make sure you take measures to make them aware of that balance and how to access the balance.

When you start to make a long term investment in anything, you probably will want to add it to the inheritance passed to your heirs. When it is a savings account, stocks, and property, it is easy to make an inventory. All those assets will be easy to track in your tax records or business ledger.

What will happen to the Bitcoins saved during multiple years if something happens to you? Remember that one of the key aspects of Bitcoin is privacy, which means the owner of a wallet can conceal his identity. If you do not talk about that with your heirs or companion, they won't know about this investment.

Even if they know about Bitcoin, it will be impossible to access the balance with no copy of the Private Keys or recovery phrase.

In the long term, it could become an incredible source of funds to pay for lots of important things for a family:

– College education

– Health care

– Real estate

Would you be willing to risk losing all the investment and keep it away from your family? I believe that no one wants to keep those funds away from their heirs, making a difference in their financial life.

What should you do? The solution for that is simple and involves adding an additional step to your recovery plan. You must find a way to let them know about Bitcoins and how to access them. For instance, you can add a handwritten copy of your Private Keys or Recovery Phrase in an envelope with your heirs' names on it.

Make sure you explain the purpose of that paper because if they are not familiar with cryptocurrency wallets, it will be hard to link them to financial assets. Besides that, you must keep those instructions accessible only by those close to you.

7.6 Horror stories about Bitcoin

Do you want to know about some horror stories about Bitcoin? There are multiple reports of people that lost huge balances of coins due to a problem with their back-ups. It is something that you should take as an example of how important it is to take it seriously.

To close this chapter, we have two stories that will show you the importance of a backup. I changed the names of both persons, but you can easily Google the story to find more about them.

7.6.1 The US$ 220 Million password

What would you do if someone knocked on your door or sent you a message asking if you would like to become a millionaire? That is something that usually happens in movies when a regular person receives such an offer to change his or her life and become a millionaire.

Usually, in the story, you have to do something dangerous or illegal to get the money. What would you do? A lot of people would not have second thoughts about it.

Would you be willing to take the chance to become a millionaire? What if I told you that you have to do something simple to get thew. Like keeping a piece of paper in a safe location for ten years?

Is that a map to a chest full of cash? No, it is a paper that has a password to decrypt the content of a hardware wallet.

Meet the incredible history of a programmer from San Francisco, California. He is an early investor of cryptocurrencies, and as a person that takes his investment to a high standard, he uses a hardware wallet to protect it. A long time ago, he got a device called IronKey and placed the Private Keys in his wallet.

During the setup process of this wallet, he got the recovery phrases. As everyone recommends, he wrote that on a piece of paper. He was doing everything right to protect his balance. What is the balance of his wallet? According to him, he has 7,002 BTC in the wallet. A quick conversion puts the value around 220 Million USD.

Can you guess what happens to the piece of paper that holds his valuable recovery phrase? As you can imagine, he lost the paper. He only had a single copy of the paper.

To make matters worst, the device he uses adds another layer of security on top of the recovery phrase. It allows you to input the recovery phrase ten times before wiping out the device contents. He already tried eight times and has only two additional guesses.

Is there a way to retrieve his balance and fortune? Unfortunately no. If he can't guess the password, he will be locked out from his Bitcoins forever. What are the odds of guessing such a password? To be honest, unless he finds the paper, it is very unlikely to regain access.

When he wrote down the password on a piece of paper a couple of years ago, the Bitcoin value was not even close to what we have today, with prices getting close to 40,000 USD and rising. That is not an excuse and shows how important it is to keep a reliable and secure way for storing your financial information.

If you decide to keep the password on a piece of paper, you should take measures to secure it and have at least three copies!

7.6.2 Bitcoins in the trash

After you have your backups ready and written on a piece of paper, you must take measures to ensure nothing happens to the copies. What if you only have a single copy of the paper, and someone finds it in your house and think it is a worthless note with random words and throw it in the trash. How happy would you be?

That was not the case with an IT manager from the United Kingdom that was an enthusiast of Bitcoin from the early days and was able to mine almost 8,000 BTC in an old laptop. It was when Bitcoin was worthless and only an experiment. Because of that, he never made a proper backup of the Private Keys from his wallet.

At some point, he sends the hard drive of that computer to the trash. Here we have two problems:

– You should not dispose of electronics in regular trash

– He didn't have a copy of his Private Keys

He is hurting the environment and his conscience for the rest of his life because those Private Keys controls a balance of 250 Million USD.

As a desperate measure, he even tried to get a permit from his city council to search the local landfill for his hard drive, with a promise of giving away 25% of his balance to the city administration.

That is another impressive example of how something simple like a backup copy of your data can make a difference. If he had a written copy of the Private Keys, he would easily import that to a software wallet and enjoy the life of a millionaire.

What is next?

With a backup and recovery plan ready, it is time to start acquiring and managing your Bitcoins. As soon as you get into an exchange to buy some of those coins, you will notice that we have many options besides Bitcoin.

What is Ethereum? How does it relate to Bitcoin?

There is no doubt that in cryptocurrency, the word Bitcoin is one of the most popular terms. A lot of people don't even know about other digital currencies that also use similar technology. In the next chapter, we will explore Altcoins' world and how you can expand your cryptocurrency experience going beyond Bitcoins.

Chapter 8 - Beyond Bitcoin: The altcoins

A word that usually appears next to Bitcoin in many ways is Altcoin. What is an Altcoin? In this chapter, we will take a look at other cryptocurrencies and how they relate to Bitcoin. You will learn about coins that mirror a fiat currency and how some try to improve Bitcoin features.

There are thousands of Altcoins available in the market, and you should take a close look at each one of them before trying to add any of them to a portfolio.

Here is what you will learn:

– The cryptocurrency ecosystem

– How to extend the value of a cryptocurrency

– What are stable coins?

– What is the Ethereum altcoin?

– What is the Litecoin altcoin?

– What is the Monero altcoin?

– Other promising coins

8.1 The cryptocurrency ecosystem

What is the most popular cryptocurrency in the world? It is undoubtedly Bitcoin that always have the headlines in newspapers and overall media. That is usually a result of the spikes in pricing. Another reason to make Bitcoin so popular is that it was the first of its kind. After a few years, a Blockchain idea to manage financial assets started to give people other insights about the technology.

New projects using the Blockchain technology started to appear with applications in multiple fields. Today we have a market with thousands of options in cryptocurrencies other than Bitcoin, offering various segments for a potential investment or transfer of value.

A quick look at the CoinMarketCap (https://coinmarketcap.com/) brings a list with an incredible amount of cryptocurrencies and digital coins (8,000). Here is a list with the top 10:

1. Bitcoin

2. Ethereum

3. Tether

4. Polkadot

5. XRP

6. Cardano

7. Litecoin

8. Bitcoin Cash

9. Chainlink

10. Binance Coin

As you can see from the list, we have Bitcoin at the top with an estimated Market-cap of 608,000,000,000.00 USD. That is, by far, the most valuable cryptocurrency on the list. It also works as the locomotive that pulls the entire market. When Bitcoin goes up, everybody else follows. The same applies in the opposite direction.

After the incredible success of Bitcoin and its open-source nature, other enthusiasts start to think of possible uses for the Blockchain technology, and new coins appeared. Some of those new coins try to mimic the purpose of Bitcoin by offering a way of store value. Of course, it is not a full copy of Bitcoin but an attempt to improve the protocol.

For instance, in the list, we have Bitcoin Cash, a hard fork of Bitcoin itself. The proposal was to make confirmation speeds faster by changing the block size for miners, making transaction processing more quickly in theory. Since the developers never reached a consensus, a hard fork from the Bitcoin network appeared.

One aspect of those coins that might confuse people is that they use Blockchain technology to ensure maximum security and reliability. Still, not all of them have a separate network. Some of the cryptocurrencies work on top of other networks as a second layer.

8.1.1 Extending the value of cryptocurrencies

The primary purpose of Bitcoin is to become a way of transfer and store value like what we have with gold. Why would someone buy and store gold? Because it is a valuable asset for thousands of years. Can we do anything other than admiring the beauty of gold? There are some applications in industrial processes and electronics, but other than that, it is just a good looking metal.

You can think the same way of Bitcoin and its main purpose, which is to store value.

Some people tried to expand the use of Bitcoin and the incredible Blockchain technology to solve real-world problems. With that in mind, we saw the birth of multiple platforms using the Blockchain and backed by a cryptocurrency.

That is the case of Ethereum, which is one of the first cryptocurrencies derived from Bitcoin. Unlike Bitcoin that is solely a digital currency, you can think of Ethereum as a software development platform. It uses a coin called Ether (ETH) to allow people to buy and trade computational power in their network.

With Ethereum, you have a separate Blockchain and miners specialized in processing ETH transactions. There are multiple other projects following a similar principle like Polkadot (POT) and Cardano (ADA).

Since most people know Bitcoin as "the cryptocurrency," all other cryptocurrencies receive the name of "Altcoins" or alternative coins. Alongside the alternative coins, we have stable coins. To make it easier to understand, we can use two main categories to organize cryptocurrency other than Bitcoin:

– Altcoins

– Stable coins

Can you hold any one of those coins in a wallet? That depends on the type of coin you wish to trade and if the wallet offers support for the token.

8.2 The stable coins

The first type of coin other than Bitcoin that you will find in exchanges and multiple locations are the stable coins. They receive this name because their purpose is to mirror a fiat currency. Since most people trade using United States Dollars (USD), some of the most popular stable coins mimic the Dollar value. Among them, we have:

– Tether (USDT)

– USD Coin (USDC)

– Dai (DAI)

– TrueUSD (TUSD)

Why would people use stable coins instead of fiat currency? The answer to this question is simple; fees. Since financial institutions and exchanges charge a fee whenever you trade using fiat currency, many people choose to use stable coins to do their business.

It is also an easy and cheap way of sending money worldwide because you don't have the substantial price fluctuations of Bitcoin, and anyone can withdraw the value to a local bank with the help of an exchange.

A concern that many people have with stable coins is their real value. If you think about it, it would be like having a company printing dollars and promising that they have the same fiat currency value.

8.2.1 Tether (USDT)

One of the most popular stable coins is Tether (USDT) that has the primary purpose of mirroring the United States Dollar value (Figure 8.1). If you look at transaction volume in a day, the Tether coin is even bigger than Bitcoin! A significant amount of people use Tether to swap and move between different cryptocurrencies.

Figure 8.1 - *Tether logo*

How does it work? The coin uses multiple different Blockchains since it doesn't have a unique network. Among the Blockchains used by Tether to secure transactions:

– Bitcoin

– Ethereum

– Algorand

Who created this coin? The Tether is from a company based in Hong Kong, which also has the name of Tether. According to the company, whenever someone buys a Tether, they will place the corresponding value in reserve to back the coin. As a result, they must have funds to cover all the supply of Tether in the market.

Unlike other cryptocurrencies that are open-source and have public-data to audit, Tether is part of a private business. There are multiple people in the cryptocurrency community raising questions about those reserves and what would happen if a massive amount of coin holders decide to cash out.

Since there is no audit data available under their records, you have to trust them. Should you use and trust Tether? Do your research before using the currency and prefer stable coins with an open-source philosophy.

Even with news of possible lawsuits and regulatory investigation, people don't seem to care and still trade massive amounts of Tether (USDT) every day.

8.2.2 USD Coin (USDC)

Another popular option in stable coins is the USD Coin that has the same purpose as Tether but with some significant differences. The coin has a value that always remains the same with a rate of 1:1 to the Dollar. One of the aspects that makes USD Coin unique is safety (Figure 8.2).

Figure 8.2 - USDC logo

Among the creators of USD Coin, we have two large companies:

– Circle

– Coinbase

They formed the Centre Consortium to manage USD Coin. They usually point to two advantages of the USD Coin:

– Audit from an external accounting company

– Regulatory compliance from Coinbase

When you compare it to other stable coins, which only claims that all existing tokens have a counterpart with fiat currency deposits, and audited solution shows much more confidence.

8.2.3 Why use a stable coin?

Why people use a stable coin instead of a balance in fiat currency? There are many reasons to use a stable coin in an exchange:

– Reduced fees

– Quickly swap to different cryptocurrencies

– Protection from price fluctuations

If you keep an eye on Bitcoins' price for a couple of days, you will notice that it changes a lot. It is by far one of the most volatile assets in the market when you think about finances. In a matter of days or hours, the price can go up or down with huge margins.

A simple way to protect yourself from those changes is to exchange Bitcoins for a stable coin. The fees are usually lower than trying to sell it for fiat currency. That is a common practice for people making day trade with cryptocurrencies.

Here is the math behind such protection:

1. Wait until the Bitcoin price reaches a limit

2. Once it starts to drop, exchange the balance to a stable coin

3. When the coin price stops falling, you can exchange it back and make a profit

This simple math is what many people try to do as a protection from the price changes.

For instance, by using a stable coin, you can quickly freeze the gains with a cryptocurrency. For example, if you have 1 BTC and the price spikes from 35,000 USD to 40,000 USD, you can trade 5,000 USD as a stable coin. It will allow you to withdraw that amount to a bank account later if you wish.

Later you can even use the stable coin profits to buy more Bitcoins if the price goes down.

Another way of using stable coins is much simpler and important, which is to send money to someone else. Have you ever tried to send money overseas? If you desire to use the traditional SWIFT or IBAN transfer, a transaction can take days to complete, and a bank can charge a considerable fee to send it.

There are faster ways to send money like PayPal, but they charge a massive fee for convenience. If you use a stable coin to transfer money, you will quickly get a minimal fee and funds in a wallet.

8.3 The Altcoins

With the success of Bitcoin in his early days, we started to see a shift in people that thought it was a great piece of technology and began to think about ways of expanding the system. Some people proposed changes to the protocol since it is open-source, and others created new projects expanding the Blockchain use.

We saw the birth of Altcoins, or also known as alternative coins. Since Bitcoin is the most famous cryptocurrency, all other currencies receive the name of alternative coin or altcoin. Even with a similar technological background, most of them have a unique or different feature from Bitcoin.

An aspect of all Altcoins that you will probably notice is that most of them try to improve, in some way, an element of Bitcoin like:

– Practical application

- Transaction times

- Fees

- Privacy

- Decentralization

Those are all features we find in the Bitcoin network, and for newcomers, they work great, but after a while, you will see that we have a lot of room for improvements.

- It is hard to use Bitcoins for anything other than store value

- A transaction in the Bitcoin network can take 20-30 minutes to complete

- Fees for small transfers are too expansive

- You can trace back the identity of a wallet owner when using an exchange

- Large mining pools are becoming a dominant force and undermine the decentralization effort

Each Altcoin tries, in its way, to solve those problems with improvements.

Besides those problems we commonly find in the Bitcoin network, we have another proposal from the Altcoins related to the currency's purpose. Unlike Bitcoin that is a store value, we have Altcoins offering a platform to create new apps running in a Blockchain.

8.3.1 Ethereum (ETH)

The first of the Altcoins to appear back in 2013 is Ether and the Ethereum network (Figure 8.3), which is more than a simple currency token but a platform that allows developers to create apps in their Blockchain. Those apps have the name of Dapps, and they use the Ether currency as a transaction fee in the network.

Figure 8.3 - Ethereum logo

It also features a unique software language and an ecosystem of already implemented Dapps. There are multiple uses of Blockchain technology to create such apps, and many people think it offers a more sustained way to grow a cryptocurrency.

Instead of using the currency as a way to move value only, you make it useful as a way of potentializing the Blockchain technology. Since developers need to pay transaction fees using Ether, there will always be demand regardless of value.

Where can you buy Ether? Since ethereum is the second most used and valuable cryptocurrency, it is available in nearly all exchanges. It is easy to buy and trade Ether.

A lot of Altcoins uses the Ethereum Blockchain with a protocol called ERC20. When you see an Altcoin with this protocol, it means the token uses the Ethereum Blockchain.

8.3.2 Litecoin (LTC)

From the Altcoins in the market, we have one that tries to mimic the behavior of Bitcoin as a way to store value, which is Litecoin (Figure 8.4). The cryptocurrency protocol works just like Bitcoin and has a separate Blockchain. One of the improvements proposed by Litecoin is confirmation time.

Figure 8.4 - *Litecoin logo*

To speed up confirmation times, the block processing time of Litecoin was cut from 10 minutes to 2,5 minutes in Litecoin. That means you can expect a confirmation time four times faster.

Since it has much faster confirmation times, it is most likely to find retailers and merchants accepting Litecoin as payment. However, coming from a world with real-time conformations, a wait time of about 2-5 minutes still seems a lot.

Another problem of Bitcoin that Litecoin tries to solve is fees for small transactions. When you start to manage Bitcoins daily, you probably will notice that fees to transfer small amounts are incredibly high. Because all fees come from the transaction size measured in bytes, you might have the same amount of fees for values equivalent to:

– 10 USD

– 10,000 USD

– 100,000 USD

That is great when you are trying to send a lot of money to another wallet, but it is terrible for small values. When paying someone a value of 20 USD in Bitcoins, you might have to pay 7 to 9 USD in fees with a quick confirmation time. It will be cheaper to send the money using PayPal.

One of the changes implemented by Litecoin is reducing the fees in the network to make it easier to work with micro-payments.

Info: *If you compare cryptocurrencies to precious metals, many people see Bitcoin as gold and Litecoin as silver.*

Should you buy Litecoin? That is hard to answer and will mostly depend on your purposes. For long term investments, you might want to look for Bitcoins as a way to store value. Remember that Litecoin doesn't have the same features as other coins like Ether running a software platform.

It means you will have to trust that people will still value the currency to keep it alive.

Where can you buy and exchange Litecoins? Like Bitcoin and Ether, you can trade Litecoin in nearly all exchanges since it is a common cryptocurrency.

8.3.3 Monero (XMR)

One of the unique tokens available today that tries to solve two common problems of Bitcoin is Monero (Figure 8.5). To fully understand the benefits of using Monero, we have to go back to Bitcoin and list those problems.

Figure 8.5 - *Monero Logo*

A key promise from Bitcoin is to allow people to make transactions with privacy in mind and no disclosure of who owns a wallet. However, with the widespread use of exchanges and the Blockchain's open-nature, it is easy to trace back a transaction and find a wallet owner.

For instance, when you register to use an exchange to trade Bitcoins and start to follow the recommendation of buying the coins and send to a cold storage wallet, an exchange can easily follow the funds. All they need is to look in the Bitcoin ledger to trace back the wallet addresses used by an account.

Since you must provide several identification checks, as part of KYC, the exchange can give that information back to anyone. It can be for marketing purposes or even law enforcement and governments if requested.

Another promise of Bitcoin is to become a decentralized network that anyone can join. In the past, that was true, and we can still find multiple nodes spread worldwide. The reality today is that we have a lot of computational power from mining pools in places with cheap electricity like China.

To solve those problems, we have the Monero (XMR) token. The main purpose of Monero is to become a truly private way of transferring value. How they do that? With Monero, you have a system that adds random data to any transaction and sometimes creates temporary addresses to obfuscate the real destination of funds.

It also uses a consensus mechanism with the name of CryptoNight, which discourages large mining farms from working in the network.

Since Monero can offer a truly private way for people to send and receive money, it is a popular choice for people to hide their financial activities. If you thought that Bitcoin was the main currency in the dark web, it is a title currently awarded to Monero.

Due to their enhanced privacy features, it is not easy to buy Monero with fiat currency, and most of the biggest exchanges doesn't support the token. You have to search for smaller exchanges that offer the token.

8.4 Other promising coins

There are thousands of altcoins available today, and most of them have no real value. Since most of the technology is free and open-source, with the right tools, you can create a new cryptocurrency in a matter of hours and place it to run in a Blockchain like Ethereum.

It is not easy to find promising new altcoins that can shake the market, but two easy bets are Polkadot and Cardano. They promise to overtake Ethereum as a base layer for applications with lots of new features and improvements.

We also have unreleased projects like the Mina Blockchain (https://minaprotocol.com), promising a lightweight network with a ledger of less than 1MB. They promise a file with only 22KB. The impacts of that are overwhelming because it can turn smartphones into full nodes of this Blockchain.

What is next?

At this point, you have all the information necessary to start using and managing Bitcoins and Altcoins. The natural next step is to register in exchange to buy your first cryptocurrencies. Ensure you follow all the security recommendations and make a backup of your Private Keys or recovery phrase.

Do your research, and you can even find some great opportunities in Altcoins!

Additional resources

For an updated list of resources and sites listed in the book, you can visit:

https://bitcoinhandbook.info

If you need assistance about a resource in the book, feel free to send us a message:

https://www.b3a.pub/contact/

Don't forget to leave us a rating or review!